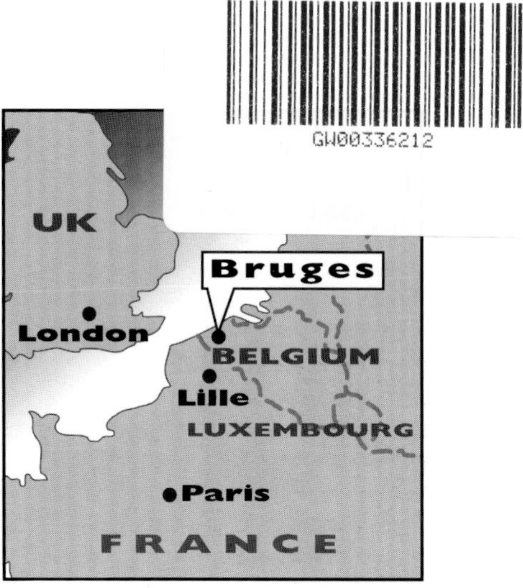

About This Guide

This guide book deals exclusively with Bruges. At last, the visitor is no longer restricted to books that devote just a few pages to what is by far the most appealing, as well as the most visited art city in Belgium.

So near to Britain, Bruges can now be reached in a multiplicity of ways, easily and quickly, including of course, via the Channel Tunnel: each is fully described in this book.

Although Bruges is a compact city, there is so much to see dispersed along its narrow streets and winding canals that several days are needed before its charms have been exhausted. Four routes are detailed enabling the visitor to see the best of Bruges, logically and comprehensively. They all begin at Markt, the central square, and end either at Markt or the bus station. Large-scale, detailed maps and precise directions mean that visitors need never lose their way. Further detailed information listing opening times, addresses and telephone numbers of points of interest, bars, restaurants and hotels is also included and will prove invaluable when exploring.

An outline of lacemaking and 'Flemish Primitive' painting, so well presented in Bruges, is given, and the reader directed to selected restaurants and bars. A map showing the location of recommended hotels and restaurants is also included. Flemish culinary specialities are explained and a selection of those fantastic Belgian beers described.

For details on How To Use This Guide please refer to page 6.

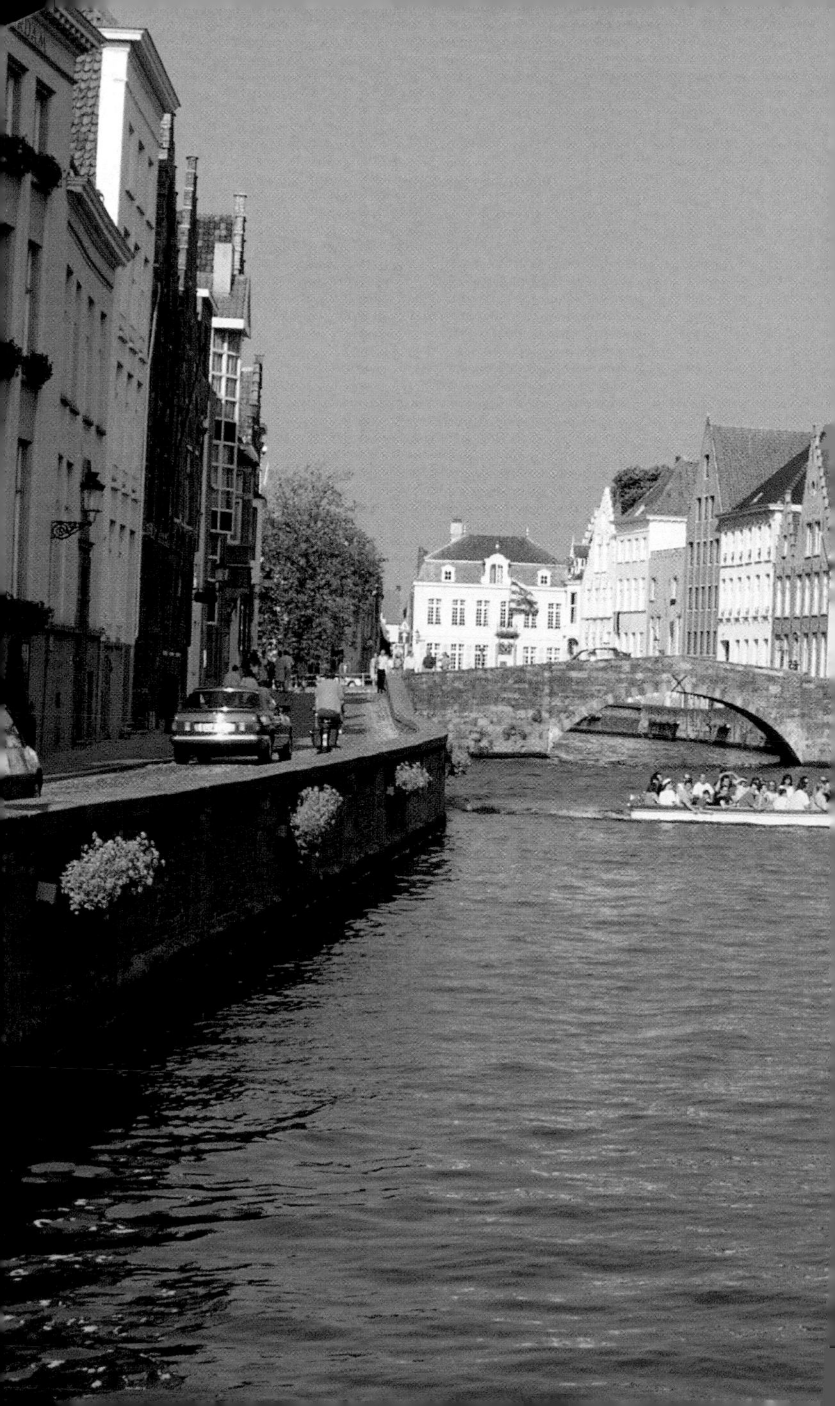

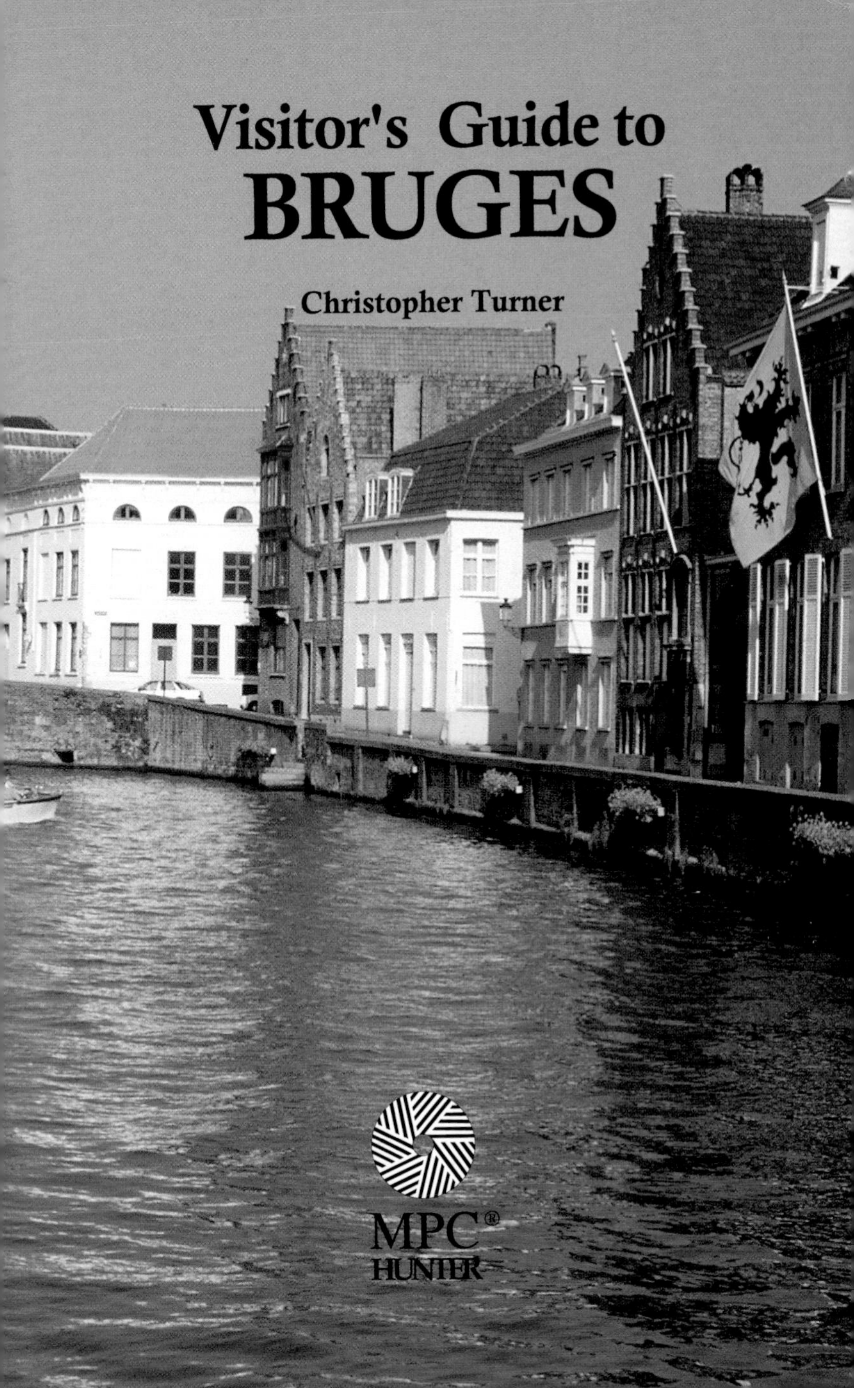
Visitor's Guide to
BRUGES
Christopher Turner
MPC®
HUNTER

Published by: Moorland Publishing Co Ltd,
Moor Farm Road West, Ashbourne, Derbyshire DE6 1HD England

Published in the USA by: Hunter Publishing Inc,
300 Raritan Center Parkway, CN94, Edison, NJ08818

ISBN 0 86190 605 5

British Library Cataloguing in Publication Data:
A catalogue record for this book is available from the British Library.

Colour origination by: ga graphics
Printed in Hong Kong by: Wing King Tong Co Ltd

Acknowledgements

The author and publisher would like to thank Robert van Loo, the Bruges Tourist Office, the City Museums Board Brugge for use of the illustration on page 47 and Pauline Owen at the Belgian Tourist Office in London.

Cover photograph: *Recently restored, Ezelpoort was the north-west exit point from the medieval city.*
Back Cover, (left): *There are many embarkation points in Bruges for the half-hour-long boat trips on the canals.* (middle): *Viewed from the Belfry, Bruges appears even more 'toytown'.* (right): *Lace is sold from many shops in Bruges.* (below): *Stadhuis, the Gothic masterpiece on which the design of many Flemish town halls is based.*
Page 2: *The Spiegelrei once penetrated further into the city, but was blocked by the construction of Jan van Eyckplein.*

Picture Credits

Illustrations have been supplied by the Bruges Tourist Office (Robert van Loo): front cover, back cover (middle and right) and pages 38, 39 (top), 42, 74-75, 115;
the City Museums Board Brugge: page 47;
bottom picture, back cover: MPC Picture Library.
All other remaining illustrations are by Christopher Turner.

Contents

KEY Symbols

- Tower/Fortification
- Museum/Art Gallery
- Church
- Parkland
- What to do if it Rains
- ✱ Other Place of Interest
- Food and Drink
- Building of Interest

How To Use This Guide

This MPC Visitor's Guide has been designed in an easy to use format. Each chapter covers a region or itinerary in a natural progression which gives all the background information to help you enjoy your visit. MPC's distinctive margin symbols, the important places printed in bold type and a comprehensive index enables the reader to find the most interesting places to visit with ease.

At the end of each chapter, an Additional Information section gives specific details such as addresses and opening times, making this guide a complete sightseeing companion.

The Facts for Visitors at the end of the guide lists practical information, including a comprehensive accommodation and eating out section, and useful tips to help plan a visit both prior to travel and during a stay.

Welcome To Bruges

The Belgian Tourist Office is delighted that this new book by Christopher Turner, is of our beautiful city of Bruges. He vividly portrays its wealth of magnificent architecture, fascinating rich museums, local crafts and fine restaurants.

We know it is a town much loved by many people, whether for a weekend break or a longer stay, and feel sure after reading this knowledgeable book a great number more will discover its delights.

They will also learn the value of all our Flemish historic cities with their vast variety over a small area — everything within walking distance on an intimate scale.

Patrick De Smaele
Belgian Tourist Office, London

FOREWORD

It was a disaster for Bruges in the fifteenth century that led to the triumph of Bruges in the twentieth. The silting up of its outlet to the sea brought to an end the status of Bruges as Europe's leading centre of trade — everything transferring, almost overnight, to Antwerp. Citizens abandoned their splendid art city, most of those who stayed falling into abject poverty.

Virtually nothing was built in Bruges for almost four centuries, and relatively little of importance was demolished. For these reasons, with the exception of Venice, no other European city has survived that can be identified so completely with the Middle Ages. Other Belgian cities have splendid market squares and cathedrals, but in none of them is it possible to observe such a completely medieval scene. Arnold Bennett, as long ago as 1896, summarized the situation perfectly, 'The difference between Bruges and other cities is that in the latter you look about for the picturesque, while in Bruges, assaulted on every side by the picturesque, you look curiously for the unpicturesque, and don't find it easily'. If anything, the truth of Bennett's appraisal has become even more apparent 100 years later. More recently, Henry Miller wrote that his visit to Bruges enabled him 'to see the world afresh with the eyes of a child'.

Some are tempted to include Bruges in a tour of either Belgium, Benelux, or even Europe, spending just one day in the city and concentrating on its major tourist attractions. If time is limited, this is understandable, but the whole point of Bruges — its relaxed, rather wistful charm — will be missed. Although from a map the city appears to be small, so many of its streets deserve to be visited that if they were all strung together the distance would be surprisingly extensive.

Four itineraries are suggested in this book, so that those spending 3 to 4 days in Bruges will see the most important locations without wasting time by doubling back on themselves or getting lost. All four begin at Markt, which is easy to locate due to its towering belfry; two of them end at Markt, and the other two end at the railway station, from where buses ply to and from the city centre. It is not intended that these itineraries should be followed slavishly, nor is it possible to indicate how long each will take. Much depends on the time spent in churches and art galleries, or at serious beer-tasting sessions (for research purposes of course) and these obviously will vary with the individual. One can undoubtedly spend at least a week in Bruges without exhausting all that it has to offer.

INTRODUCTION

History

Towards the close of the Roman Empire, *Gallia Belgica,* a Roman province incorporating the Netherlands, was invaded from the north by a Germanic army; this proved unable to penetrate through the great forest that then existed between the Rhine and the North Sea, and a frontier was established. Thus was created the Germanic north of Belgium and the Romanised south, a divide which is still manifest, primarily by language difference: the north of Belgium 'including Bruges' speaking Dutch and the south speaking French. Only a vestige of the great forest has survived; it is known as the Zonienwoud and lies to the south of Brussels.

Following the break up of Charlemagne's Empire in 843, Flanders, an area that included what are now the provinces of East and West Flanders (Belgium), Zeeland (Holland) and Nord (France), fell under the control of counts that were the vassals of the French kings. Boudewijn, 'of the Iron Arm' the first Count of Flanders, built a fort to protect Bruges from Norse raiders, thus establishing the city. By tradition, the first living creature that Boudewijn saw in the region was a bear, which is why the city's coat of arms incorporates this animal. The name of Bruges may have derived from *brug* (bridge), although an alternative, the Norse word for a landing place, is equally possible. In the eleventh century the counts of Flanders gradually extended their territory east of the River Sheldt, acquiring what had been German possesions. Bruges was made the capital of Flanders in 1089, but it was 40 years before the first canal/rampart defences encircling the city were begun.

A great storm known as the Dunkirk Flood created the Zwin estuary in 1134; the River Reie flowed into it from Bruges, and virtually overnight the city had become a navigable port, with direct access to the North Sea.

It seems likely that the Romans had introduced sheep to the region, and Flemish weavers became supreme as clothmakers. Initially, local wool was used, but it soon became apparent that wool from England, with its longer, silky fibres, produced a better quality cloth. Trade with England became all important to Bruges, and eventually the city obtained a monopoly on English

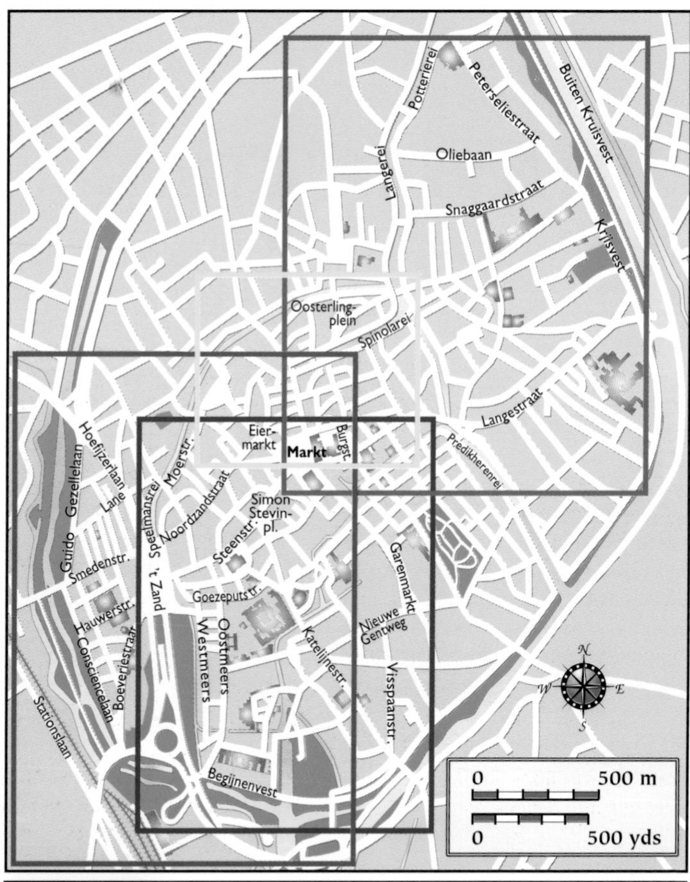

map index		Page
Introduction	Hotel and Restaurant Street Plan	**14**
Chapter 1	Highlights of Bruges	**26**
Chapter 2	North-East Bruges	**78**
Chapter 3	North Bruges	**102**
Chapter 4	South-West Bruges	**122**

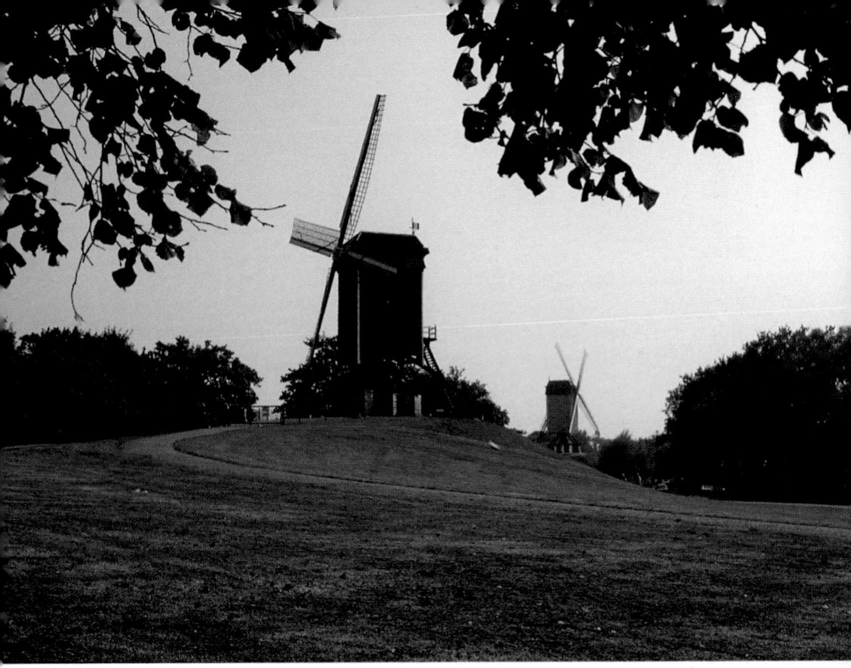

Three windmills stand on the ramparts of Bruges, only one of which is operating

wool — in 1282 it was established that only cloth made from English wool could be designated 'first class'. Unfortunately for Flanders, England and France had become deadly enemies, but although the Flemish were obliged to give tacit support to the King of France, to whom they owed allegiance, they maintained commercial ties with England. In order to safeguard the English wool trade, Edward I invaded, occupying much Flemish territory; however, he soon had to return home to 'hammer' the Scots once more, and Philip the Fair immediately reclaimed the land that Edward had captured. Philip constructed the second defensive 'envelopment' of Bruges in 1297, creating a double ring of canals and ramparts around the city.

In 1302, the Flemish trading guilds decided to put an end to French interference, and their members fought successfully against the trained soldiers of France, defeating them in the streets of Bruges ('the Matins of Bruges'), and at the Battle of the Golden Spurs. Two years later, the French were defeated for a third time at the Battle of the Pevelenberg. Flanders had won a measure of independence, and trade prospered, partly due to its strategic location between the Mediterranean and Scandinavia. Eventually, around twenty mercantile nations were represented in Bruges, all with their own trading houses, and some with their own weigh-houses.

In 1384, Flanders ceased to exist as a defined region, due to its incorporation into the Burgundian dukedom following the death of the heirless Count of Flanders, Louis de Male. His daughter, Margaret, had married the Duke of Burgundy, Philip the Bold, in 1369, and he therefore added Flanders to his exisiting territories. Although the Burgundians spoke no Dutch, their period of rule, which lasted for less than a century, marked the golden age of Flanders.

However, it was Philip the Good (1396-1467), who became Duke in 1419, aged 23, transferring his capital from Dijon to Bruges, that was primarily responsible for the preeminence of the city. He greatly expanded his dukedom, either by force or by purchase, until, in 1443, the Burgundian Netherlands had acquired the dimensions of present day Belgium, Holland and Luxembourg combined. In spite of his sybaritic fondness of luxury and art, Philip was an opportunist, bent on extending his power. Together with Henry V of England, he signed the Treaty of Troyes in 1420, by which England and Burgundy were ceded large areas of France. Subsequently, Philip befriended Edward IV during the late stages of the Wars of the Roses, sheltering him in Bruges, and supporting his return to the throne. Politically, however, Philip wished to remain on good terms with Charles, King of France, and refused to give Edward effective military support against him. Eventually, Philip even attempted to acquire Calais from England for his dukedom.

Charles the Bold inherited the dukedom from his father in 1467. He married Margaret of York, Edward IV's sister, and maintained the friendship between Burgundy and England. Unlike his father, however, he did not court good relations with France, battling continuously with Louis XI. As a complete turn around, Edward IV subsequently formed an alliance with the French King, fighting against whom, Charles was killed at Nancy in 1477, and as he left no male heir the dukedom of Burgundy effectively came to an end. His daughter Mary, who only survived her father by 5 years, married Maximilian of Austria and the Hapsburg rule of Bruges began.

Maximilian's tax measures against the citizens of Bruges led them to revolt in 1488, and they imprisoned him in Markt for 22 days. This political unrest, combined with the silting up of the Zwin estuary, presaged the downfall of Bruges, and foreign merchants were soon leaving in droves for Antwerp.

Persecution of Protestants by the bigoted Spanish Hapsburg rulers Charles V and his son Philip II, led to further strife, in which the northern Netherlands broke away to form a separate Protestant state (Holland), whilst the southern Netherlands remained Catholic under Hapsburg rule. The frontier, established by the Treaty of Munster in 1648, was arbitrarily delineated where the military activity had ended, and it remains to this day.

The fortifications of Bruges were strengthened in 1614, bastion towers being erected for the first time. Ten years later, a canal link with Ghent was established. Nevertheless, the seventeenth century saw Bruges in decline, virtually all its trade having been transferred to Antwerp. It is surprising that Charles II, the exiled King of England, should have spent 3 years in the city (1656-59), an indication, perhaps, that some vestige of prosperity in Bruges remained.

Throughout the eighteenth century, the southern Netherlands was given scant regard by its distant Hapsburg rulers, whether from Madrid or, as from 1713, from Vienna. In 1786, an English visitor to Bruges reported that there were so few inhabitants to be seen that the city looked as though it had been depopulated by the plague.

Bruges was occupied by Napoleon's army in 1795, full of anti-religious revolutionary zeal. Churches and monasteries were stripped of their treasures, most of which were sent to Paris, from where, for almost 20 years, Bruges would be ruled. After Napoleon's defeat at Waterloo (south of Brussels) in 1815, the Netherlands were reunited under the Treaty of Vienna. Sadly, in spite of good intentions, 236 years of separation had increased the differences between the north and south to such a degree that amicable reunification proved impossible. The south Netherlanders rebelled in 1830 and a separate state — Belgium — was born, Prince Leopold of Saxe-Coburg, a favourite uncle of the future Queen Victoria, being invited to rule. Surprisingly, Bruges was made capital of West Flanders province, even though around half its inhabitants were by then in dire poverty.

Help, however, was not far distant, its provider coming from an unexpected quarter, Bruges's old trading partner, the English. Sentimentally visiting the Waterloo battlefield, many of them had passed through Bruges, and been struck by its antiquity. In 1820, the poet William Wordsworth recorded 'a deeper peace than is in deserts found'. His sister Dorothy found its 'inhabitants are accordant with the stateliness of former ages'. During the later Victorian era, the British acquired a deep love of all things medieval, a love that was expressed in their art, literature and architecture — Gothic was very much in vogue.

Very soon, news about the romantic antiquity of Bruges spread in Great Britain, and a colony of British expatriates settled in the city, encouraging local architects to restore, or even to build anew, in Gothic Revival style. As a country, Belgium had become prosperous under Leopold II, even founding — rather late in the day — its own empire, the Belgian Congo. The port of Zeebrugge was built between 1895 and 1907, linked to Bruges by a canal, and Bruges once more had a maritime capability, albeit a limited one. The city ex-

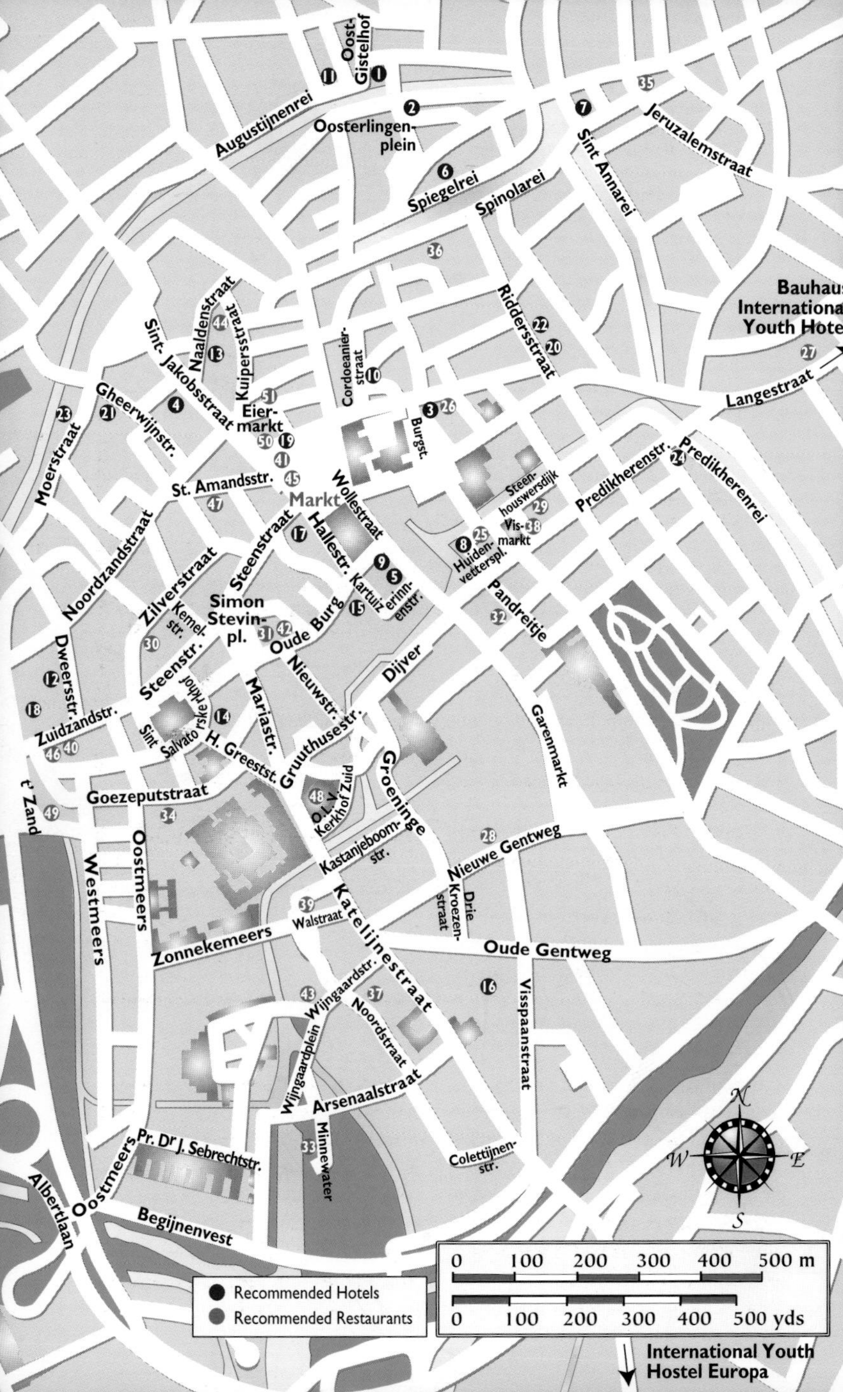

Oost-Gistelhof
Augustijnenrei
Oosterlingen-plein
Spiegelrei
Spinolarei
Sint Annarei
Jeruzalemstraat
Bauhaus International Youth Hotel
Langestraat
Ridderstraat
Naaldenstraat
Kuiperstraat
Sint-Jakobsstraat
Cordoeanier-straat
Burgst.
Eiermarkt
Gheerwijnstr.
Moerstraat
St. Amandsstr.
Markt
Wollestraat
Hallestr.
Steenstraat
Noordzandstraat
Predikherenstr.
Predikherenrei
Steenhouwersdijk
Vismarkt
Huidenvetterspl.
Kartuizerinnenstr.
Pandreitje
Zilverstraat
Kemelstr.
Simon Stevinpl.
Oude Burg
Nieuwstr.
Dijver
Dweersstr.
Steenstr.
Zuidzandstr.
Sint Salvatorskerkhof
Mariastr.
H. Greestst.
Gruuthusestr.
Groeninge
Garenmarkt
t' Zand
Goezeputstraat
O.L.V. Kerkhof Zuid
Kastanjeboomstr.
Nieuwe Gentweg
Oostmeers
Westmeers
Walstraat
Katelijnestraat
Drie Kroezenstraat
Zonnekemeers
Oude Gentweg
Wijngaardstr.
Wijngaardplein
Noordstraat
Vispaanstraat
Arsenaalstraat
Minnewater
Pr. Dr J. Sebrechtstr.
Colettijnenstr.
Oostmeers
Albertlaan
Begijnenvest
N
W
E
S
0 100 200 300 400 500 m
0 100 200 300 400 500 yds
Recommended Hotels
Recommended Restaurants
International Youth Hostel Europa

KEY

Four Star Hotels	Restaurants Over 2,000 BF
1 Brughe (ter)	25 Duc de Bourgogne
2 Bryghia	26 Kapittel ('t)
3 Holiday Inn Crowne Plaza	27 Karmeliet (De)
4 Navarra	28 Snippe (De)
5 Orangerie (De)	29 Swaene (Die)
6 Relais Oud Huis Amsterdam	30 Zilveren Pauw (Patrick Devos)
Three Star Hotels	**Restaurants 1,200 - 2,000 BF**
7 Adornes	31 Bhavani
8 Duc de Bourgogne	32 Braamberg (Den)
9 Grand Hotel Oude Burg	33 Kasteel Minnewater
Two Star Hotels	34 Lotteburg
10 Cordoeanier	35 Paspartout (De)
11 Europ	36 Spinola
12 Imperial	37 Tanuki
13 Lucca	38 Visscherie (De)
14 Salvators	**Restaurants 700 - 1,200 BF**
15 Voermanshuys ('t)	39 Begijntje ('t)
One Star Hotels	40 Belle Epoque
16 Ibis Brugge Centrum	41 Central
17 Koffieboontje ('t)	42 Keteltje ('t)
18 Putje ('t)	43 Maximilian van Oostenrijk
'H' Grade	44 Oud Brugge
19 Central	45 Sint-Joris
20 Patritius	**Restaurants Below 700 BF**
Guest Houses	46 China
21 Mrs Deloof	47 Due Venezie (Le)
22 Mr and Mrs Gheeraert	48 Michelangelo
23 Mrs Nyssen	49 Pallieterke ('t)
24 Mrs de Vriese	50 Raadskelder
	51 Voske Malpertuus ('t)

panded well outside its ramparts, and a railway station was built.

In 1892, Georges Rodenbach wrote *Bruges-la-Morte* (*Bruges the Dead*), and visitors flooded from the ports of Ostend and Blankenbergh to see this unique north European example of a petrified medieval city. Gradually, throughout the twentieth century, tourism increased until it became by far the most important industry in Bruges. Fortunately, the romantic British immigrants had already impressed on Brugeans the importance of conservation, and strict town planning controls were introduced as early as the nineteenth century.

Although occupied by Germany during both World Wars, Bruges fortunately escaped physical damage, and its almost completely ancient appearance was undisturbed. Jealous accusations that the city has become an insipid 'theme park' do not really bear examination. Some buildings may have been somewhat over-restored or prettified excessively, but most examples of this are the result of nineteenth century over-enthusiasm. Moreover, it should be remembered that Bruges in its heyday was a city of crisp brickwork and fresh paint — as it is now — and those that would prefer to see it otherwise must surely be suffering from an excessive 'pleasure of ruins' romanticism. Conversely, most will find that the real upsetters in Bruges are the few modern buildings that have been permitted — particularly the hotel and municipal office block in Burg, on the site of the old cathedral, and the hotel in Oude Burg, behind Halle.

Bruges, in spite of its inundation by tourists in the city centre, is an extremely popular place in which to live. Crowds of Brugeans descend on any centrally-located house that comes on the market, and peer through the windows as if a particularly gruesome murder had recently been committed within. This is because Brussels can be reached within the hour, and Eurocrats, including many from Britain, prefer to live away from the capital. Bruges is far from being a lifeless museum city.

The Brugeans, their Religion and their Language

The great majority of Brugeans come from Flemish stock, with Germanic origins, as do 60 per cent of all Belgians. They tend to be serious-minded, but don't allow the work ethic to interfere too much with their leisure pursuits. All schoolchildren in Belgium have Wednesday afternoons free, and a tradition has evolved that doting fathers, whenever possible, also take Wednesday afternoons off to spend with them.

It will be noticed that two physical types prevail: one short, round-faced and chubby providing a startling contrast with the other, tall, thin and lantern-jawed (as depicted by Van Gogh in some of his early portraits of mining families painted in Belgium). Most are Catholic, but the faith seems to be on the wane if Mass attendances are anything to go by. However, religious-inspired festivals (particularly if a holiday is involved) are supported enthusiastically. Almost everyone speaks English well, and is highly literate. In spite of anti-Brussels diatribes from certain British politicians, and football hooliganism from certain football supporters (memories of violence during the Bruges/Chelsea match will take long to fade), British visitors are treated with particular affection, gratitude for the assistance given to Belgium in both World Wars, and the consequent friendships made, seem to be passed down through the generations. It is also the British that still, in spite of an unrealistic exchange rate, provide the majority of visitors who stay overnight in Bruges.

The official name of the language spoken in Bruges is Dutch, not Flemish, although it is sometimes referred to as such. Apparently, Flemish Dutch is a rather antique version of the language, but there are no communication difficulties between Dutch-speaking Belgians and Dutch-speaking Dutch. Surprisingly, it is sometimes impossible for a citizen of Bruges to understand a citizen of Ghent, the nearest large town, that speaks the local dialect. The word Dutch evolved in the Middle Ages from Dietse or Duutse, meaning 'the language of the people'. Deutsch (German) has the same source. Visitors will note that locally the city is called Brugge, but for some reason the French version, Bruges, has been adopted by English-speaking people. Yet we manage to call its modern port, correctly, Zeebrugge, not Zeebruges — how convoluted is entymology!

Tourism is, of course, by far the most important industry in Bruges, and one would expect the residents to become a little tetchy with the hordes of camera-clicking visitors, who never seem to know where they are, or where they are going, and find the place names completely unpronounceable. But miraculously, all are greeted by the Brugeans with a friendly smile, and given well-considered information, even at the end of a busy summer season. If a conversation is struck up in a bar, it is quite usual for a tourist to be offered a drink — without one being expected in return.

Food and Drink in Bruges

Basically, there are three types of restaurant in Bruges: fast food outlets, tourist restaurants and luxury establishments. Only a few bars (or cafés as they are usually called) offer much in the way of food. Belgian cuisine, at its upper level, is basically French, with a few local specialities incorporated. Some of the best food in the world is served in Belgian restaurants, and those who can afford their understandably high prices are recommended to have at least one 'gourmet' meal during their stay in Bruges.

Whilst menus at the more expensive restaurants are usually written in French, astonishingly, many restaurants aimed primarily at tourists display menus outside their establishments in Dutch, a language that the vast majority of prospective customers do not understand. One can only presume that nationalism plays a part here, as it certainly makes no commercial sense. Some may have noticed a similar attitude in Barcelona, where menus in the Catalan language are displayed to uncomprehending tourists. The only remedy seems to be to walk on, or demand to be shown a menu in English or French — and still walk on.

Many will wish to take the opportunity of sampling Flemish speciali-

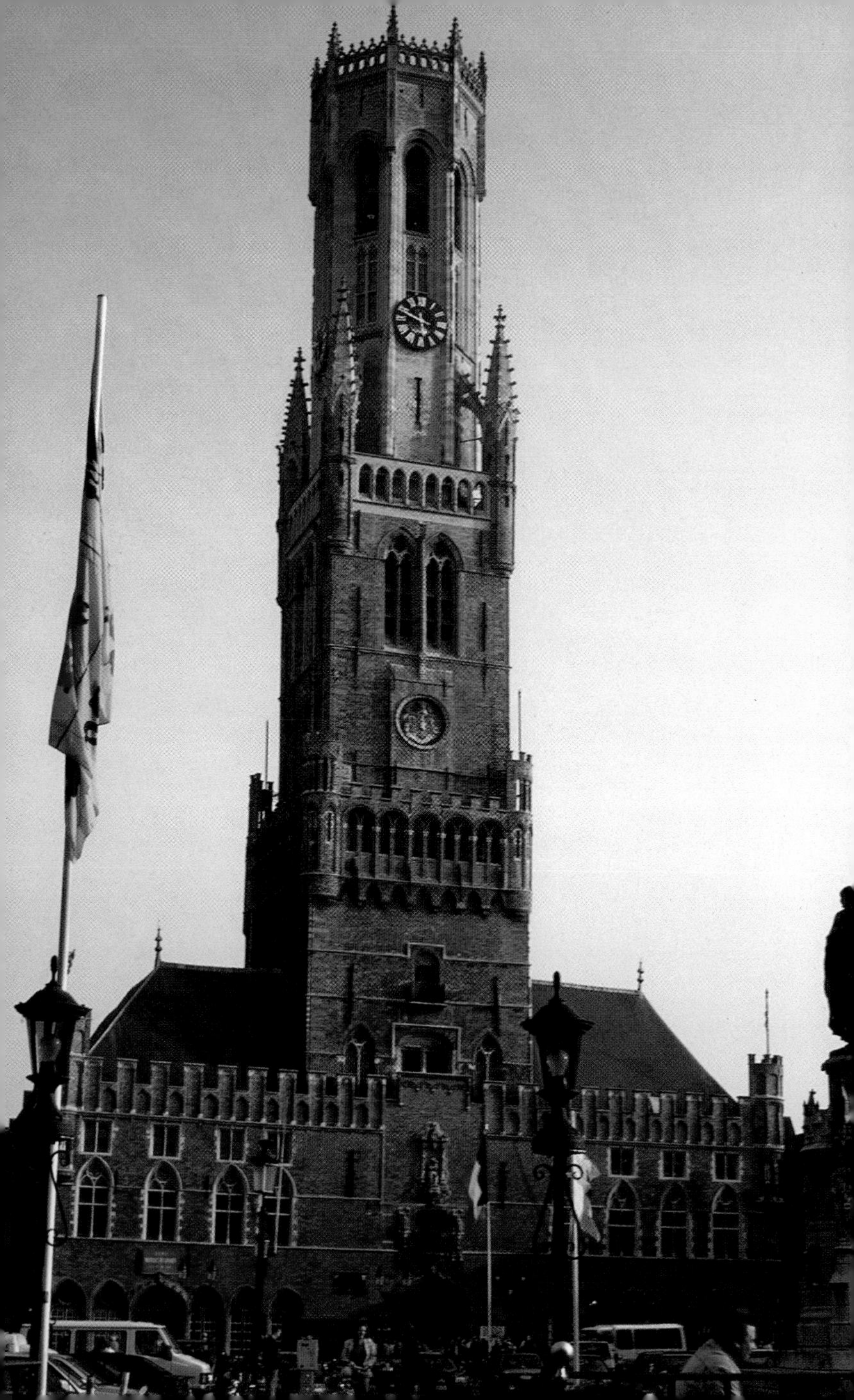

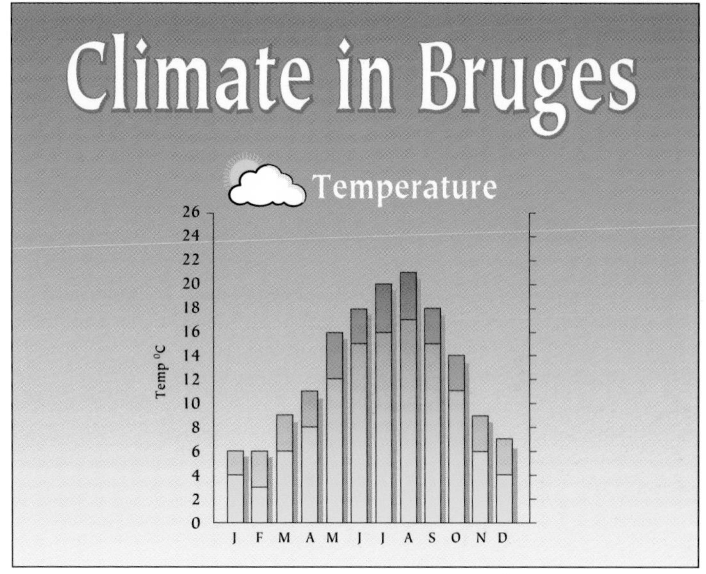

ties, which are only available in Belgium. These are absolutely delicious, particularly the casseroles (*carbonades*), simmered in beer, but only generally available outside the summer months.

The great culinary feature of Bruges, also outside the summer months, is mussels — always, but always, served with a mountain of *frites* (chips). Whilst Belgians may eat mussels two or three times a year, it seems to be expected, at least in Markt, that tourists want to consume nothing else. Very few of the luscious molluscs will have ever been to the seaside, virtually all come from Holland, where they are farmed in salt-water lakes, and can attain a huge size. Unfortunately, they do not seem to have quite the sweet, slightly fishy flavour of mussels from the open sea. No less than one kilogram weight per person is served: expect to be charged at least 500BF. Ask the waiter if the mussels are *Jumbo*, the largest and tastiest variety.

Two Flemish favourites not to be missed are *Waterzooi*, a chicken or fish dish from Ghent, prepared in a thick, rich white sauce. It is often served in two separate portions so that the dish remains hot. Equally delicious is wild rabbit simmered for around 90 minutes in white beer — *Konijn op grootmoeders wijze* (rabbit grandmother's style). Prunes or rai-

Facing page: Bruges to most is identified by its towering Belfry, constructed in stages over several centuries

sins are often cooked with the dish, but the only vegetables involved are onions; bread or even cake may be used to thicken the sauce. Do not allow chips to be served with this as they are a poor accompaniment; make it clear that boiled potatoes or bread are preferred. It is not usual to accompany the dish with vegetables, but apple sauce is sometimes served.

Carbonade a la Flamande is simply a casserole, usually of beef, to which beer is added. *Hutspot a la Flamande* involves vegetables, and can be compared with a Lancashire hot-pot, although the meat is more likely to be beef than lamb. *Stamppot Ardennaise met Worst* is a thick stew served with spicy sausage — an Ardennes speciality that occasionally appears on Bruges menus. Although not a Flemish dish, *Blan-quette de Veau* is extremely good in Belgium (for those who are not squeamish about eating veal). Cheese is rarely served in Bruges restaurants, but if the opportunity occurs, the brave should try *Herve*, a Belgian cheese that when ripe is one of the strongest in the world.

For desert, apple tart and chocolate mousse seem to be the most popular dishes or, of course, ice cream. Ice cream is very good in Bruges, and, if bought in an ice cream shop, significantly cheaper than in the United Kingdom, or France for that matter. Also cheaper than elsewhere, although still expensive, are Belgian handmade chocolates, available in Bruges from many specialist shops. Try the champagne truffles — the plain chocolate version is best.

If conversation with a Belgian ever starts to flag, just raise the subject of beer. Eyes will sparkle, lips smack, and encyclopaedic knowledge will be imparted. More than 300 beers are produced in the country — a delight for the epicure. Just about every taste seems to be catered for; from weak to strong, light to heavy, sour to sweet — even those who prefer a nice cup of tea can have a tea-flavoured beer.

In general, the more esoteric the beer, the higher the price will be, and those who wish to try them should not plan on a cheap pub crawl. Several books have been written on the wonders of Belgian beer, which is a very complex subject. Not all visitors, it must be admitted, will like the rather egregious flavours of some varieties, particularly the sour, fruit-flavoured *lambics*, and the highly alcoholic, rather sweet tripels. It is best to explain to the barman the type of flavour preferred and leave it to him. Perhaps everyone should at least once try a raspberry-flavoured *lambic*, a *trappist* — on draft if possible — a tripel (very sweet) and a *Duvel* (on the strong side). Those who are happy with a frothy, continental lager should just ask for a Pils, it will be very good — and much cheaper.

Those who have enjoyed the seventeenth-century brown bars in Amsterdam, with their sanded floors, lofty ceilings and ancient barrels, will be disappointed to learn that the Bruges equivalents are far less venerable in appearance. De Kogge comes the closest. Although the interiors of Bruges's better restaurants are exquisite, little attention is paid to the bars. Perhaps beer drinking is considered too serious an exercise to bother about the decor.

A list of recommended restaurants and hotels in various price categories is given on pages 131-133 and 136-139.

Climate

The climate of Bruges is maritime, with no great extremes of temperature. It can rain at any time of the year, but winter rainfall tends to be low. Temperatures are generally a little below those of southern England, as Flanders derives little benefit from the Gulf Stream.

Highlights of Br

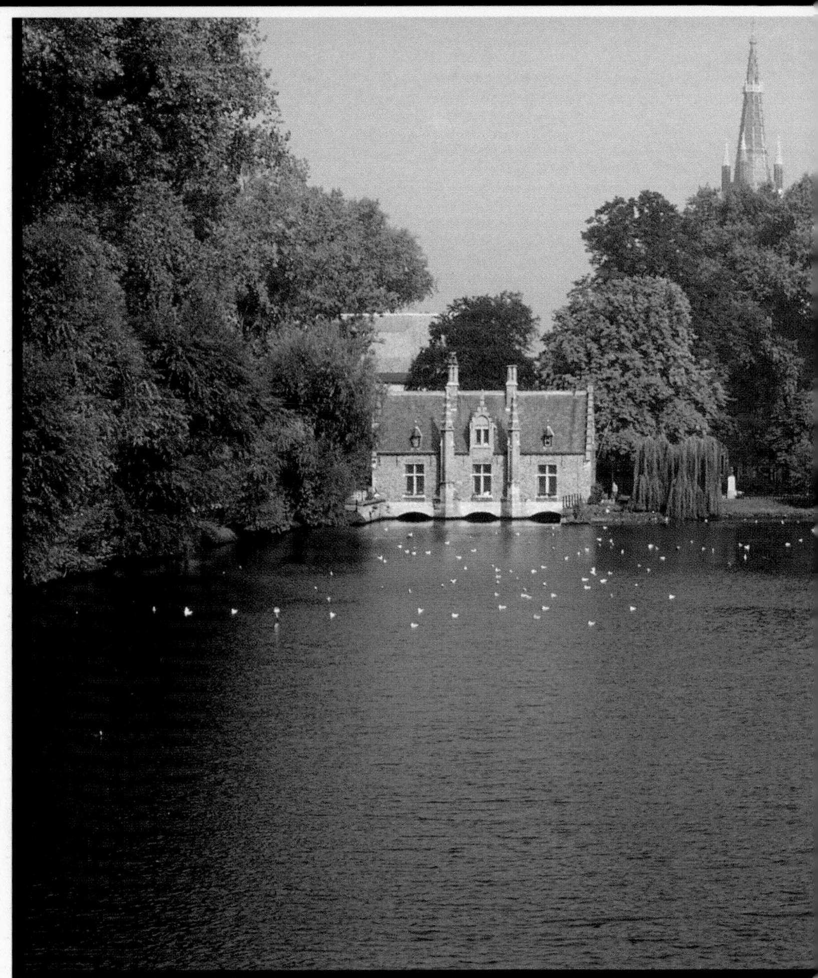

ges

1

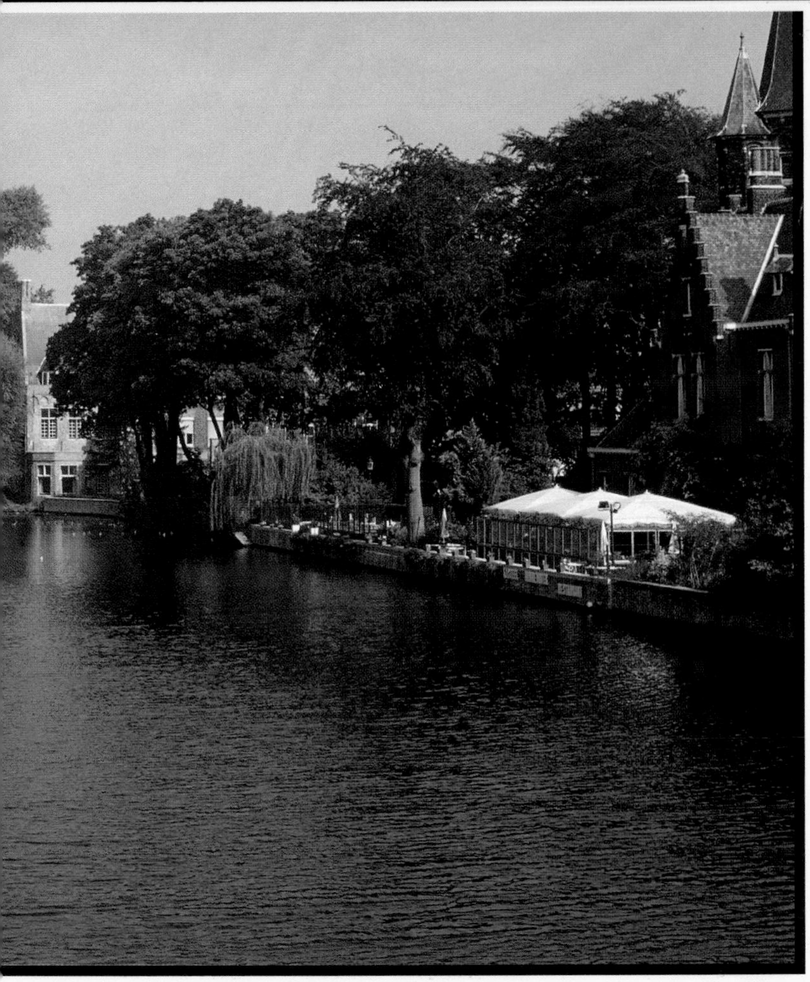

Belfry, Town Hall and the Museums

Bruges, together with Paris and Amsterdam, has become one of the most popular 'City Break' short holiday destinations for British visitors. Most, therefore, have limited time available, and, particularly if on a first visit, they may understandably wish to explore the city's major attractions as soon as possible. Conveniently, these can be seen by following an almost straight line from the Markt/Burg axis southward towards the station, from where buses or taxis depart in the direction of most Bruges hotels.

Although the distance involved is little more than 2 km (1 mile), there is so much to see that if some time is spent in all the museums and churches on route, it will be quite impossible to complete this 'itinerary' in one day. When the weather is fine and time permits, it might be a good idea to begin by exploring Markt and Burg thoroughly, as described, putting on one side the museums, including the Groeninge Museum, the city's most famous, in case the weather deteriorates. Four more important museums, plus the Church of Our Lady, are to be found, virtually on top of the Groeninge, which will prove to be particularly advantageous on a rainy day — and it can rain in Bruges at any time of the year. If at all possible, the Begijnnof and Minnewater, which follow, should be seen in fair weather. Throughout the city will be seen the Gothic letter b, usually in the form of stone plaques; this, of course, is the initial letter of Bruges, and many examples are extremely ancient.

Virtually all first-time visitors to Bruges make their way immediately to its largest square, Markt, in order to crane their necks at the belfry, rearing up from the south side. Actually, Markt (and similarly Burg), is angled north-west to south-east; this means that not only the belfry but the almost equally renowned town hall in Burg only receive direct sunlight during the late afternoon, which is, therefore, the best time to photograph them.

Locals call the **Belfry**, Belfort or De Halletoren (The Hall Tower), but whatever it may be called, the 83m (272ft) high bell tower is hard to miss; thankfully, however, it is not quite so omnipresent as the postcards and picture books of Bruges might suggest.

At the foot of the belfry, the building known as **Halle** (Hall) originally served as a cloth hall; immediately below this ran a canal, from which bales of cloth could be unloaded under cover. Modelled on Lakenhalle, a similar building at Ypres, Halle was begun towards the end of the thirteenth century, in early Gothic style, and from the outset incorporated a belfry. Initially, only the range of Halle facing Markt was

Preceding pages: Known as the Lake of Love, Minnewater's tranquil waters originally served as a harbour

built, its other three wings being added later.

The earliest belfry was probably made entirely of wood, but soon (circa 1240), a brick structure took its place. This, however, was struck by lightning in 1280, and a new belfry of stone was built between 1282 and 1296. It was bravely decided that the new, second stage should lean 1m (3ft) to the west, in order to counterbalance the lower level, which had already developed a similar lean to the east. The four corner turrets were added in 1395 as lookout points.

Designed in the late-Gothic style of Brabant, the octagonal lantern was added between 1482 and 1486, and surmounted by a decorative wooden spire. Destroyed by lightning in 1493, the spire was rebuilt in 1501, but burnt down again in 1741. This time, the lantern was left flat-topped — perhaps the insurance premiums demanded for yet another spire had become unacceptable! Eventually, in 1822, the present stone parapet was added.

There are four faces to the clock, the mechanism of which dates from 1680. Every quarter of an hour, tunes are played on the carillon, a comforting favourite being *Land of Hope and Glory*. The belfry has long been, of course, the symbol of Bruges, its 'Eiffel Tower' so to speak, and most will have seen numerous photographs of it well before arriving. Not everyone has admired the belfry, however: G.K. Chesterton, for example, disparagingly compared it with a giraffe's neck. Conversely, the American poet Longfellow praised the tower enthusiastically in a short poem dedicated to it. After a while in Bruges one gets used to the gawky structure peering unexpectedly through gaps in the roofline, rather like a spindly maiden aunt keeping a watchful but affectionate eye on her young nephews and nieces. This affection will soon be reciprocated.

The cobbled **Markt**, as its name suggests, was originally the most important market square in Bruges, and indeed it remained so from 985 until quite recently, when the Saturday market was transfered to 't Zand. Brugeans protested strongly, carrying black flags through the square on 27 August 1993, the day that the market finally closed. One cannot help but feel that they were right. It seems incongruous that the Brugeans, who have guarded their unique architectural heritage so assiduously for the sake of us all, should have allowed this European showpiece to serve as a giant car park. Similar market squares, in Brussels and Ghent, for example, have been made car free. However, the Wednesday market has been transferred from Burg to Markt.

It will be seen that the venerable Halle and its belfry occupy the entire south side of the Markt, and virtually all the north side facing it, similarly accommodates ancient buildings. Most of these were formerly the seventeenth-century guild houses of various trades, and have been converted comparatively recently into tourist restaurants. Like so many of them, Le Panier d'Or is step-gabled, its upper step surmounted by a guild

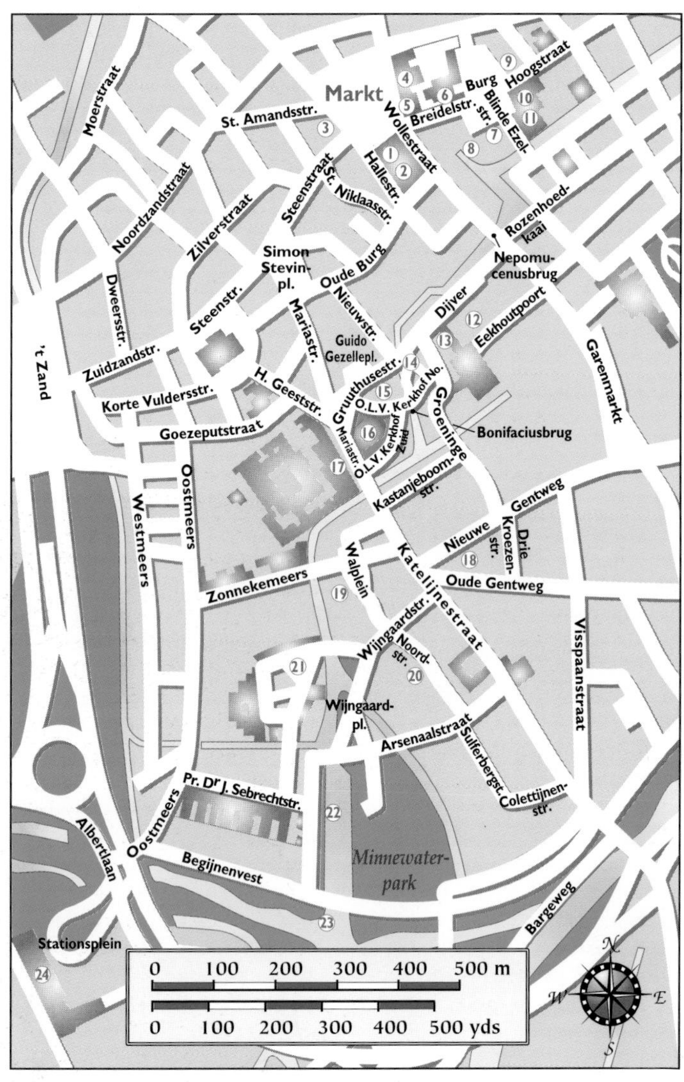

emblem, here the basket of the Tilers Guild. Further west, now La Civière d'Or restaurant, the castellated former house of the Fishmongers Guild is dated 1622: fish were sold outside the premises until 1745. Most Brugeans stick their noses up at most of the Markt cafés, considering

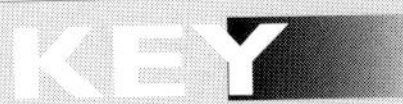

1. Belfry (Belfort)
2. Halle
3. Huis Bouchoute
4. Provincial Government (Provincaal Hof)
5. Post Office
6. Former Provost's House (Proosdij)
7. Town Hall (Stadhuis)
8. Holy Blood Basilica (Heilig Bloed Basiliek)
9. Holiday Inn Crowne Plaza Hotel
10. Bruges Tourist Information
11. Former Recorder's House (Oude Griffie) and Brugse Vrije Museum
12. College of Europe (Europacollege)
13. Groeninge Museum
14. Brangwyn Museum and Lace Museum (Kantmuseum)
15. Gruuthuse Museum
16. Church of Our Lady (Onze-Lieve-Vrouwekerk)
17. St John's Hospital (Sint Janshospitaal) and Memling Museum
18. Godshuis Meulenaere and Godshuis Sint Jozef (almshouses)
19. Straffe Hendrick (brewery)
20. Het Godshuis De Vos (almshouses)
21. Beguinage (Begijnhof)
22. Minnewater
23. Powder Tower (Poertoren)
24. Railway Station and Bus Terminal

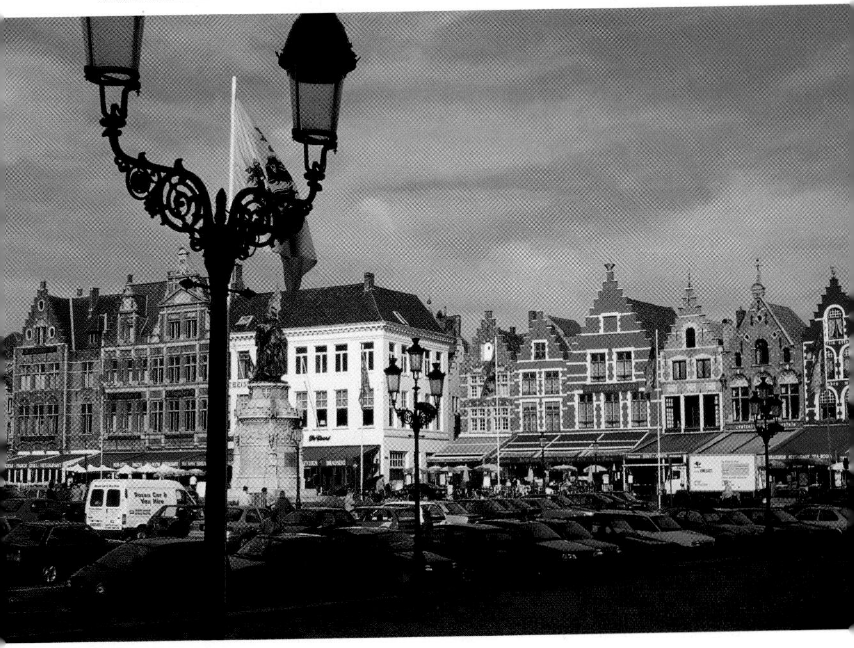

Many of the gabled houses on the north side of Markt retain emblems of the guilds that formerly occupied them: most are now restaurants, primarily aimed at tourists

them far too tourist-orientated, both in price and quality, for them to patronize. Outside the summer months, it would appear that few patrons are expected to consume anything but mussels and chips. Many British are disconcerted by this combination, which, incidentally, is also popular in Holland and France. If bread is preferred, it will, of course, be served, but the price quoted for mussels includes chips, and no reduction can be expected.

Late nineteenth-century green bronze statues of two Brugean heroes, Jan Breydel, Dean of the Butchers Guild, and Pieter de Coninck, of the Weavers Guild, who led an amateur force in the uprising against the professional French army in 1303, stand in a small green towards the north end of the square. On the monument's pedestal, a frieze depicts: the Bruges Matins of 18 May 1303, the Battle of the Golden Spurs 11 July 1302 and the Battle of the Pevelenberg in 1304. Corner sculptures represent the Belgian cities of Bruges, Ghent, Ypres and Kortrijk. Until demolished by anti-Christians during the French Revolution, the medieval church of St Christopher occupied an island site approximately where the monument now stands.

The east side of Markt is entirely pastiche Gothic, its three buildings being commissioned by the state. At the north end, built of grey sandstone (always referred to in Bruges as blue sandstone), the Burgundian Gothic style building, now the of **headquarters of the Public Works Department**, only dates from the 1920s. Much more impressive is the gleaming white **Provincaal Hof**, the seat of the West Flanders Administration, and was designed in 1878 by Louis Delacenserie. He pinched several motifs from the Gruuthuse mansion, which he had restored, in particular its slender turrets, parapet and dormer windows, and seems to have taken a liking to the Gothic turrets of the Stadhuis, reproducing them almost exactly. Finally, in contrasting red brick, we have the main post office of Bruges.

Before 1878, when it burnt down, a late-eighteenth-century, Louis XVI style range had occupied the site of these buildings. Prior to this, however, another cloth hall, known as Waterhalle, stood here, from 1294, so-named because it had been built on a bridge over the Kraanrei Canal. The hall was demolished in 1787 and the arm of the canal filled. Two of its columns survived and have been re-erected in Arentspark.

The west side of Markt is similarly dominated by Gothic Revival buildings. One, however, is genuine Gothic, although it looks even more modern than the others. This is **Huis Bouchoute** on the Sint Amandsstraat corner, a rectangular house built around 1480, its façade, combining brick with grey paintwork, having been restored in 1995, apparently with great fidelity, later roof top crenellations being removed. The ground floor now accommodates a card and souvenir shop. Still displayed is an octagonal compass; this was fitted to a weathervane on the roof in 1682 so that merchants would know the all-important wind direction prevailing.

The **Craenenburg** café was built on part of the site of an eponymous medieval house, which had a brief period of importance in Flemish history. Rioting citizens, furious at his tax impositions, placed Archduke Maximilian under house arrest within the building in February 1488. Allegedly, the captors commissioned the famous artist Gerard David to paint scenes on the shutters for Maximilian's pleasure, but there is no evidence for this. After 22 days, the Archduke was released on the promise of respecting the people's rights, but within a few weeks, his father, Emperor Frederick III, marched into Flanders to exact revenge, moving the administrative centre from Bruges to Ghent, and transferring much of the city's trade to Antwerp. The café boasts some attractive stained glass and brass chandeliers but, as is ususal in the tourist sectors of Bruges, sitting (or standing) at the bar is not permitted.

An impresive façade distinguished the adjoining **Huyse Die Maene** restaurant (*huyse* being the old Dutch spelling of *huis*, which means house). In spite of its venerable appearance, however, the building only dates from 1947.

Apart from the belfry and the courtyard of **Halle**, no interiors of the buildings in Markt are of exceptional interest. The ground floor rooms of Halle are frequently open to the public for art exhibitions, when entry to them is gained directly from the square; the Gothic vaulted ceilings remain within the rooms, but there is little other detailing of architectural interest. If the weather is clear, those who feel fit enough for a steep climb may now wish to proceed towards the archway in the centre of Halle; from the balcony above it, public announcements were made until 1769.

Immediately after passing through the archway the internal courtyard of Halle is entered. In the Middle Ages, Venetian merchants sold spices here. The side wings of Halle were added in 1365, but the south wing, enclosing the trapezium-shaped courtyard, was not built until 1566, when the Renaissance style had taken over from the Gothic. The galleries overlooking the courtyard are all Renaissance work. In the south gallery, seats have been fitted so that the public may listen in comfort to the belfry's forty-seven-bell carillon concerts. It is considered that the bells are most clearly heard in Bruges from within this courtyard — no charge is made to attend.

The former cloth hall, on the first floor, is now used for private functions, and only rarely may the public gain admission. It was at one of these functions, the opening of the College of Europe's new term, 20 September 1988, that the guest speaker, Mar-

Following page: No doubt this water pump is meant for horses only — another customer approaches

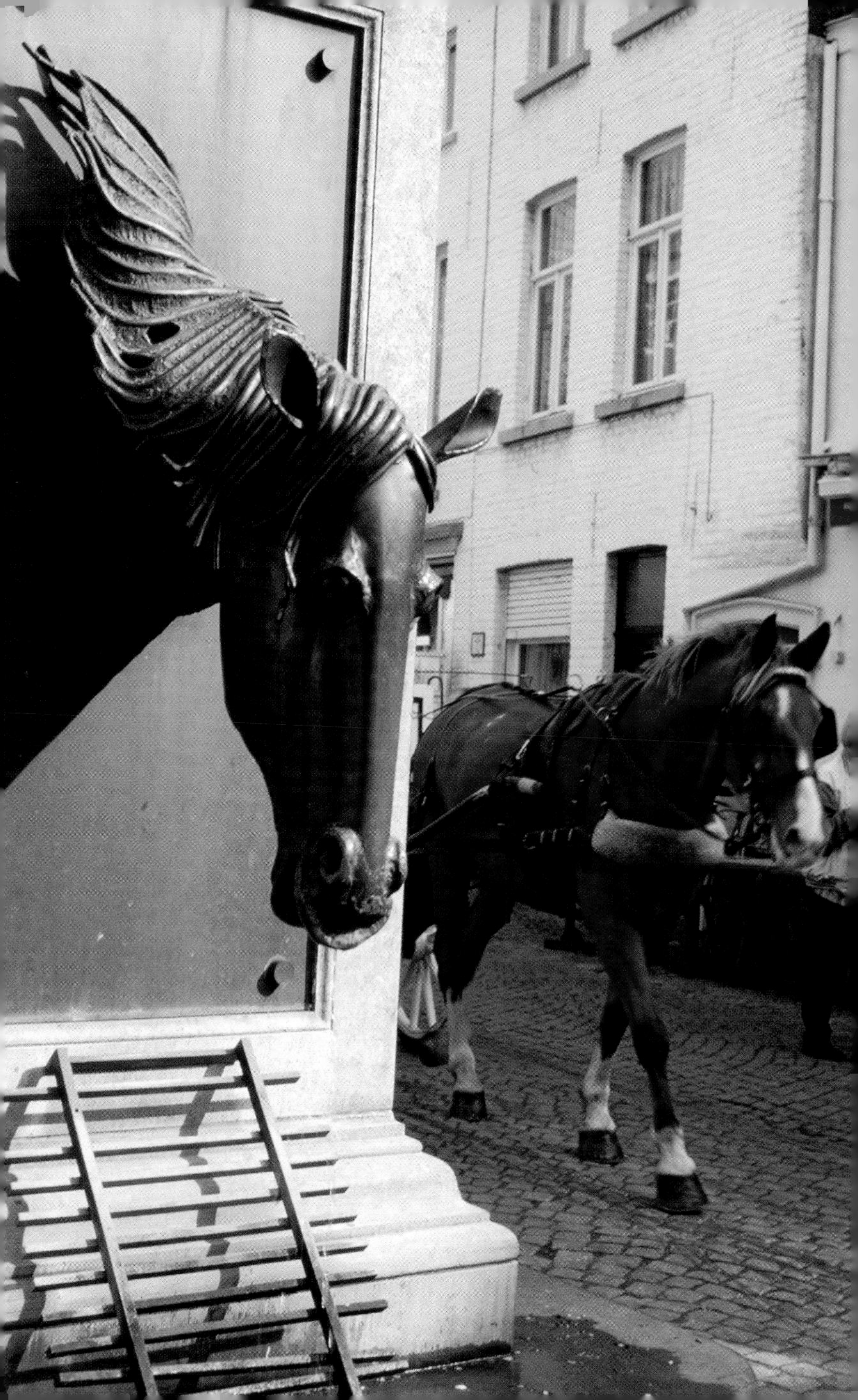

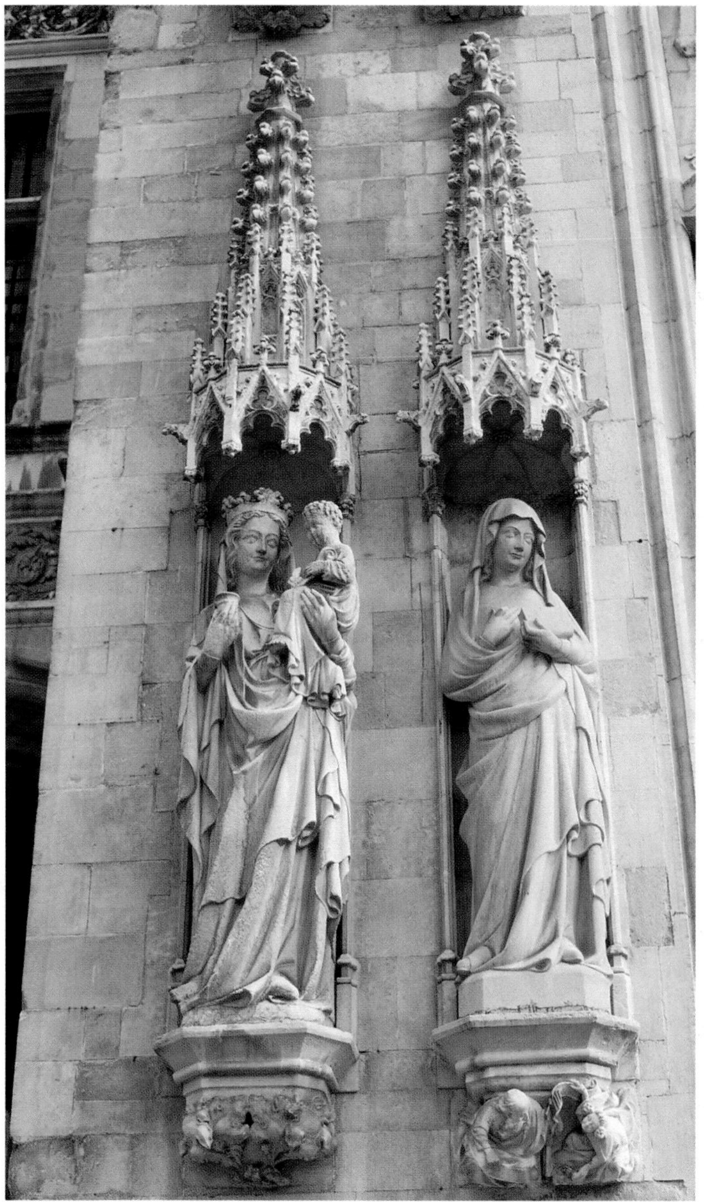

garet Thatcher, then Prime Minister of the United Kingdom, spoke against European federalism, thus giving rise to the formation of the 'Bruges Group' of British Members of Parliament that shared her views.

Access to the **Belfry** is gained from the north gallery. There is no lift, and the 366 steps, which spiral around the interior of the tower, must be climbed to reach the top — fortunately, there are resting stages. Those who have some misgivings about the safety of the structure, on account of its double lean already referred to, will be relieved to know that columns were inserted in 1554 to give structural support, and no further movement has been observed.

Kept for centuries within a room at the second stage of the belfry, called the *secreet comptoir*, was a chest containing documents known as the Privileges of the City, in which the city magistrates spelled out the rights of the citizens of Bruges. So important were these privileges considered to be that the chest was protected by an ornate double grille, fitted with nine elaborate locks, the key to each being guarded by separate officials. It is known that the grille was made by a Brugean smith in 1292 specifically for the room, which had just been built.

Views of Bruges from the top of the belfry reveal the city in all its 'toy town' charm; they are usually at their clearest and most extensive in the late afternoon. If the day is exceptionally clear, it is possible to observe the Belgian coast to the west.

After descending, a return through the arch from the courtyard into Markt, followed by an immediate right turn, leads to Breidelstraat, named, in spite of the updated spelling, to commemorate Jan Breydel, whose memorial has just been seen in Markt. Between two lace shops at numbers 12 and 14 Breidelstraat, a quaint alleyway leads to **De Garre**, a small café, popular with tourists but of no particular interest apart form its sequestered location. **Jan Brey-del-De Coninck**, at 24 Breidelstraat is still regarded by many as the restaurant where the best mussels in Bruges may be found.

On the north side of Breidelstraat, the former **House of the Provost** of the old Cathedral of Bruges (Proosdij van Sint Donaas) was constructed in the Flemish Baroque style in 1666. The building extends into the square known as Burg.

Burg in Dutch means castle, and it was on part of the site of the present square that Boudewijn, the first Count of Flanders, constructed his fortress in 862 as a defence against the Vikings, thus laying the foundations of the city of Bruges. Nothing whatsoever survives of this, but it would certainly have been Roman-

Preceding page: The present statues on the façade of Stadhuis are modern replacements of nineteenth century figures, which weathered badly and were themselves substitutes for the originals, destroyed by iconoclasts following the French Revolution

esque in style, with thick castellated walls pierced by small, round-headed windows and archways.

Only the cars of important municipal officials may be parked in Burg, and fortunately these are usually few in number. The cobbled square is significantly smaller than Markt, but includes three buildings of outstanding historic interest. Occupying most of the south side is the medieval Town Hall, which is linked by a bridge room over a narrow street with the Renaissance façade of the Old Recorders House. Attached to the west side of the Town Hall is the medieval Holy Blood Basilica; its fanciful entrance, together with the rest of the west range, is entirely pastiche Gothic. Tours of Bruges by horse drawn carriage are begun nearby. Trees now grow on the north side of Burg, but it was here that St Donaas Cathedral stood for centuries, until demolished after the French Revolution. The east side of the square is entirely occupied by a Classical complex of municipal buildings, eighteenth-century work but uninspired.

The great pride of Burg for more than 500 years has been **Stadhuis (Town Hall)**, the first municipal headquarters of its type, which was to influence the appearance of many similar structures in Belgium: those of Brussels, Ghent and Leuven being outstanding examples. Built between 1376 and 1420, of white sandstone, a material rarely seen in Bruges due to its high cost, the façade is virtually a sculpture gallery, members of the nobility and biblical figures standing within niches protected by Gothic canopies. It was the biblical figures in particular that infuriated the French revolutionaries, but just to be on the safe side, they smashed all the original forty to pieces. It is known that originally each example had been gilded and painted, the great Flemish artists living in Bruges at the time, including Van Eyck, probably contributing to their decoration. In the nineteenth century, replacements were made, but the stone used proved to be too soft, and by 1960 most detail had 'melted' away. A proposal to replace them with figures of modern design having been narrowly defeated, the present set was made in a vaguely Gothic style; canopies appear to be similar to the originals. One nineteenth-century figure was considered to be in good enough condition to keep: the example on the far right of the façade. It will be noted that the present statues are undecorated, and the effect must be very different from the riot of colour that existed in medieval times.

Stadhuis is entered primarily to admire its Gothic Hall, with the world-famous timber roof. Large paintings of the rulers of Bruges and Flanders decorate the ground floor hall. A bluestone staircase leads to the Gotische Zaal (Gothic Hall) on the first floor.

Of the many important events in Flemish history that have taken

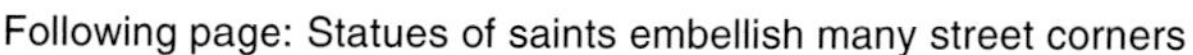

Following page: Statues of saints embellish many street corners

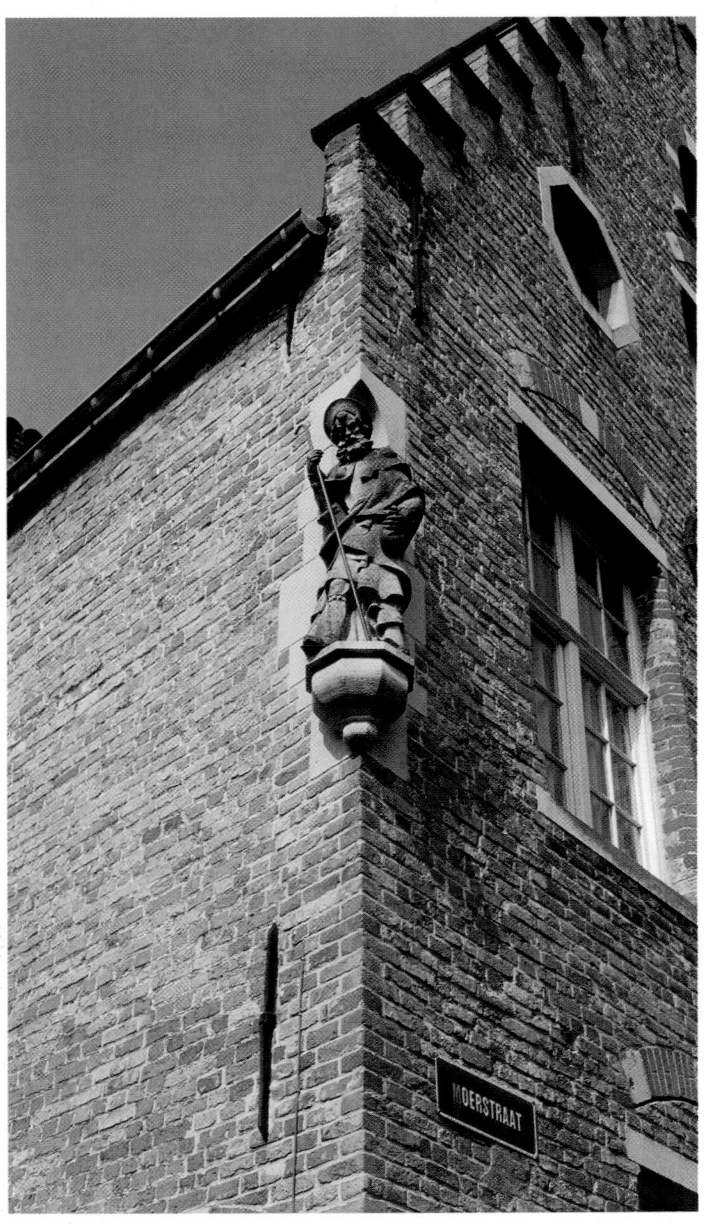
MOERSTRAAT

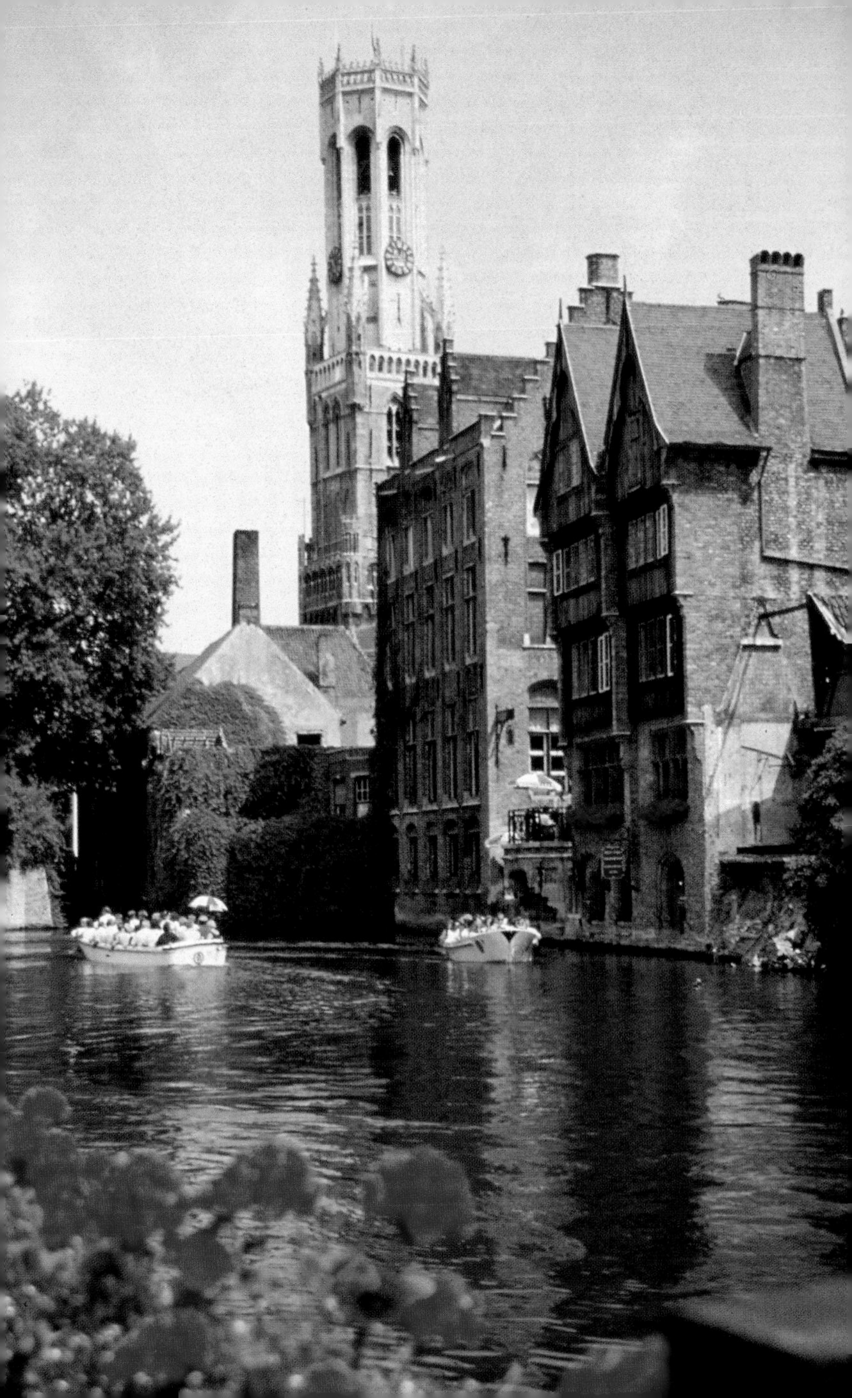

place in this great room, the best known is the Assembly of the States General of the Netherlands in 1464. Constructed in 1402, an unusual double vault has been employed in constructing the roof, both vaults being supported by stone corbels (also known as consoles or brackets); the vaults meet in the centre to form pendants, and thus provide a single span roof — quite an engineering feat.

Each of the sixteen corbels is carved to depict, respectively, the months of the year and the four elements; the bosses of the pendants illustrate Old Testament scenes. It would appear that all the woodwork is original, but restoration of the gilding and paintwork has taken place periodically. Visitors will be given a leaflet that identifies the medieval events depicted in the hall's murals, which only date from around 1900.

In a side room are displayed ancient maps and topographical paintings of Bruges. Also on view are sections of the Stadhuis façade's original canopies, carved by Jean de Valenciennes, who is also believed to have been responsible for the decorative scheme of the Gothic Hall's roof.

A left turn immediately after leaving the building leads to the **Heilig Bloed Basiliek** (Holy Blood Basilica), the north wall of which adjoins Stadhuis. Originally, a narrow street separated the two buildings, but this disappeared when Stadhuis was extended across it in the fifteenth century.

Although short, the much-altered north wall of the basilica does much to illustrate the complex history of this relatively small church, the most ancient building in Bruges to survive. Since constructed in 1139, the basilica has always comprised two superimposed oratories. It is believed to have been founded as the chapel of the Counts of Flanders, whose residence stood nearby, and on completion, relics of St Basil, then kept in St Donaas church, were moved to it. They had been brought to Bruges from the Holy Land in 1100 by Count Robert II of Flanders, who took part in the First Crusade. St Basil was greatly venerated in the early Greek Church, and his relics (four vertebrae), were greatly valued. Their importance, however, was eclipsed in the following century by the arrival of an even more valued relic, a rock-crystal phial purported to contain blood washed from Christ's body at the Crucifixion by Joseph of Aramathea (the Holy Blood). It is now generally believed that this was despatched to Bruges circa 1204 by Boudewijn, Count of Flanders, who had been appointed Emperor of Constantinople that year.

Fronting Markt, the first section of the north wall of the basilica's lower oratory, now attached to Stadhuis, was formed in 1504, when

Preceding page: The great view of the Belfry from Rozenhoedkaal — as every visitor remembers Bruges

a south chapel was added to the chancel for the exclusive use of lawyers. This is followed by a section of the original twelfth-century wall, with one Romanesque, round-headed window and part of another visible; a Lombard frieze has been entirely lost. The now-blocked archway that opened out from the north aisle of the lower oratory into the square was created by iconoclasts during the French occupancy. At first floor level may be seen the Gothic windows of the upper oratory.

Originally, the entire church had been built in Romanesque style, but around 1480 it was decided to completely rebuild the upper oratory, the late-Gothic style being adopted for it. During the French Revolution period, the basilica was used for storage, and became derelict; it is said that demolition was threatened but Napoleon intervened. By standing further back in the square, the unusual turrets of the basilica, which were built in the fifteenth century, come into view.

The large, arcaded porch was rebuilt in 1829, in picturesque neo-Gothic style. Entrance from here to the lower oratory is through the portal to the left, built in 1534.

Small windows and massive walls immediately announce that this is a Romanesque building. The nave is aisled but not the chancel, which is austerely provided with priest's seats (sedilia) fitted into blind arcades on both sides. The relic of St Basil, once displayed here, can no longer be seen, as it is now kept in the closed north chapel of the chancel, built for the lawyers. In the south aisle of the nave, the Virgin and Child was carved in 1300.

A south chapel was added to the nave's south aisle in the thirteenth century and, surprisingly for the date, this was also built in a matching Romanesque style. Within is displayed a figure of the enthroned Christ, which is still carried in religious processions; it was made in the seventeenth century for Jeruzalemkerk.

An archway from the chapel to the south aisle is fitted with a tympanum depicting a scene that probably illustrates the baptism of St Basil. This archway had been the priests' entrance to the church before its south chapel was added; their houses at the time abutted this side of the building.

The original public entrance to the basilica has also been relocated, as is indicated at the west end of the nave, where a blocked archway in the wall marks its original position. Access to this was from a street, which, like that at the east end of the building, has since been built over.

A late-Gothic staircase, constructed in 1523, leads to the upper oratory, where the crystal phial of holy blood is kept within a silver tabernacle presented by Albrecht and Isabella of Spain in 1611. On

Following page: Viewed from the Belfry, Bruges appears even more 'toytown'

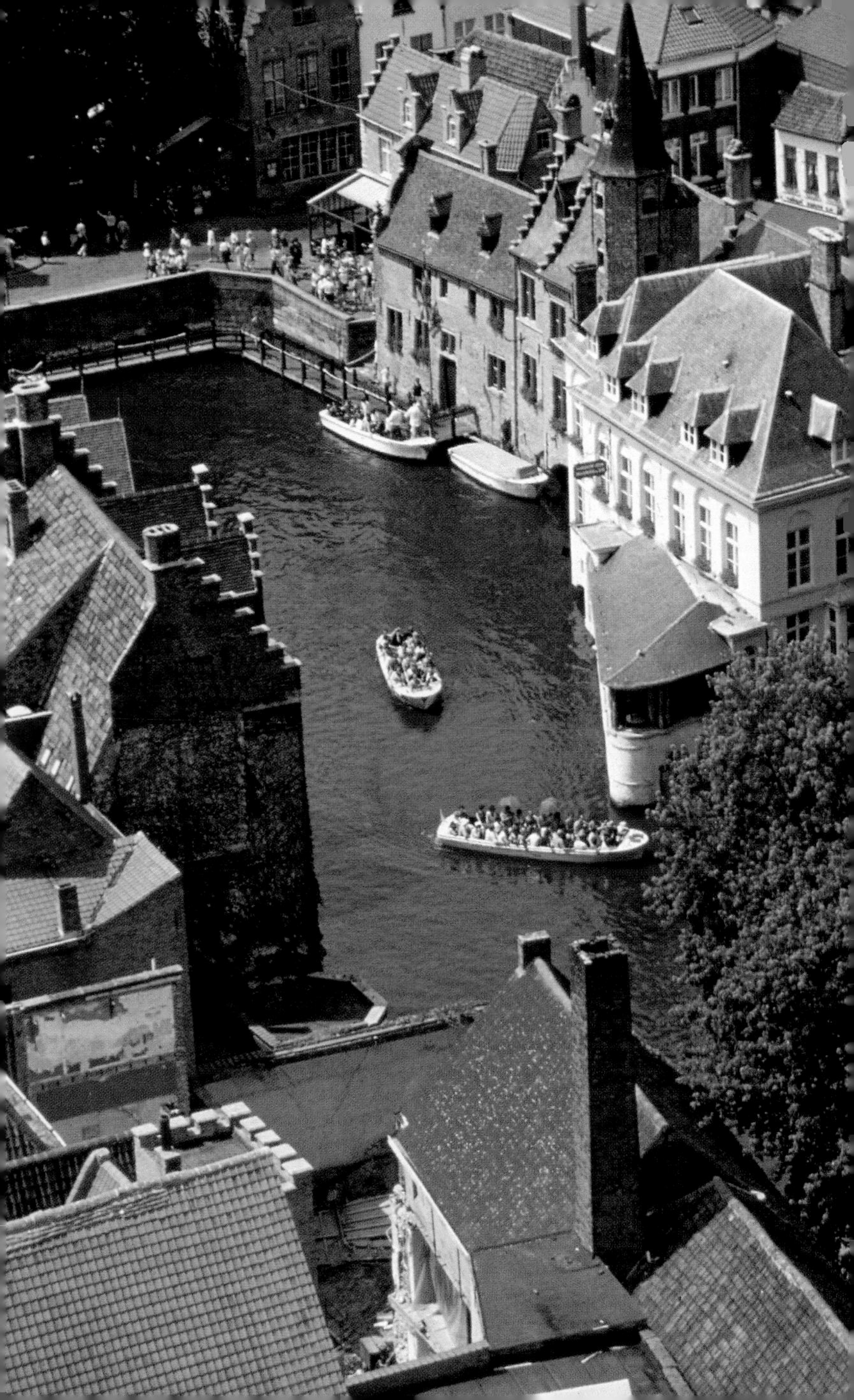

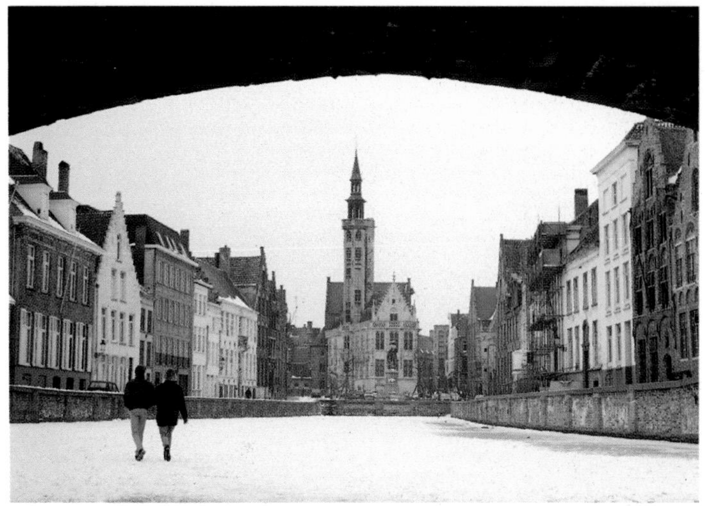

In winter, particularly after a snowfall, the frozen canals of Bruges evoke medieval paintings

The Gothic Hall of Stadhuis retains its ancient timber roof, still decorated in the original colour scheme

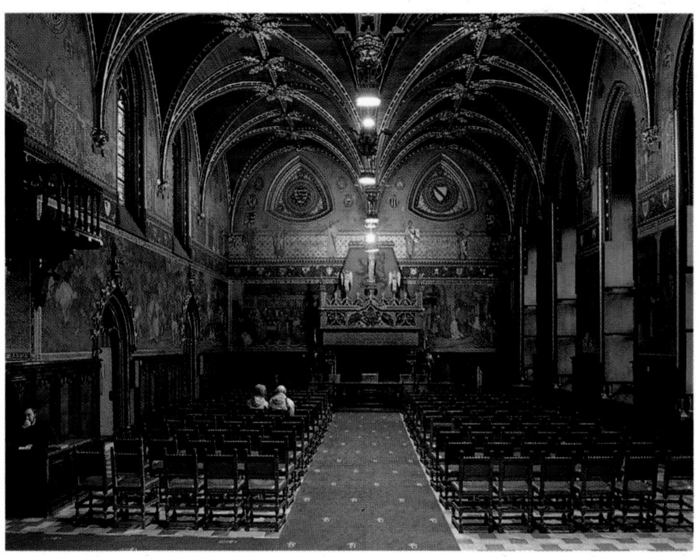

Fridays, the relic is moved to the south chapel, where it may be venerated 8.30-11.45am and 3-4pm. The phial, within its gold reliquary, is paraded through the streets of Bruges on Ascension Day, a tradition confirmed by papal bull of Clement V in 1310. It is said that on the first Friday following the arrival of the relic in Bruges, the dried blood miraculously liquified; it continued to do so from time to time, always on a Friday, but the last recorded occasion was in 1325.

It may be noted that the three archways separating the south chapel from the nave are round-headed; they are genuine Romanesque work, and all that remains of the original upper oratory. Little also remains of the Gothic reconstruction carried out in the late fifteenth century, due to damage caused during the French Revolution, which necessitated the rebuilding of the chancel in the late nineteenth century. Dating from this period are the heavy murals, but the pulpit, in the form of a globe, was carved from a single piece of oak in 1728.

Adjacent to the upper oratory is the Treasury, now a museum. Here is displayed the processional gold reliquary of the Holy Blood. It was made by Bruges goldsmith Jan Crabbe in 1617, and incorporates a diamond that is believed to have belonged to Mary Stuart of England, and the crown of Mary of Burgundy.

After descending to Burg, a left turn leads to **Mallebergplein**, a small park created at the north end of the square. Trees and benches make this a pleasant spot in which to relax on a warm day. A bronze sculpture *The Lovers* is a reminder that civil weddings take place in Stadhuis, opposite. Formerly, the park's area was occupied by the original cathedral of Bruges, consecrated to St Donaas. Rebuilt several times, the cathedral in its final form stretched eastward from the Provost's House to the west end of Burg. It originated as a tenth-century Carolingian church, which burnt down in 1184. A scale model in stone, showing how it would have appeared, with its centrally placed, circular nave, has been erected in the park. An adjacent stone slab commemorates the alleged murder in its chancel of Count Charles the Good by a nephew of the cathedral's provost in 1127.

Part of the lower level of the church was excavated between 1931 and 1990, and incorporated within the basement of what is now the **Holiday Inn Crowne Plaza Hotel**, overlooking the park. Visitors are welcome at any time to view the remains of the church, which are reached by descending the stairs to the left of the reception desk. It is helpful to examine the plan facing the bottom of the stairs before entering the excavated area. A painting of 1690 is displayed, depicting the large Gothic building that the small Romanesque church eventually became. Jan van Eyck, the painter, was buried in the cathedral in 1441. During the period of the French Revolution, all churches were secularized but not necessarily destroyed if an alternative use for the building could be found. In this instance, the cathedral was sold as national property in 1792, but demolished 7 years later.

As already mentioned, the east side of Burg, comprising **Municipal Offices**, is not particularly distinguished, the sandstone building, commissioned by the Brugse Vrije, being the work of an Amsterdam architect Jan Verkruys (1722-27). Brugse Vrije (Liberty of Bruges) was the administrative authority for the area of Flanders between the rivers Ijzer and Scheldt but excluding the city of Bruges itself. Old paintings depict a much more picturesque complex of buildings on the site, dating from the fifteenth century. Most of this complex was replaced by the eighteenth-century building, however, the rear façade, looking over the water, was spared, and its Gothic gables are seen later. The French abolished the Brugse Vrije in 1795, but its buildings survived, becoming the Gerechsthof (Law Courts) from the late eighteenth century until 1984, when it moved to a new location. Municipal offices now accommodated include the Bruges Tourist Information Office (see Facts for Visitors, page 142).

Linked to Stadhuis by the bridge-room over Breidelstraat, the façade of **Oude Griffie** (Former Recorder's House) is far more impressive. It was constructed by Jean Wallot (1535-37) to accommodate municipal records, and is an interesting architectural blend of Gothic and Renaissance features. Medallions above the ground floor columns depict Flemish rulers, while, at upper level, gilded statues of Justice flanked by Moses and Aaron are apparently accurate nineteenth-century reproductions of the originals, which were destroyed by French iconoclasts in 1792.

Oude Griffie's rooms are not open to the public, but the doorway, left (number 11a) leads to the **Provinciaal Museum Het Brugse Vrije**, accommodated within two of only three rooms that have survived from the Gothic complex: the Aldermen's Room, the Drawing Room and the former chapel. Outside the Aldermen's Room are displayed municipal items of historic value, but it is the Aldermen's Room itself (built 1520-25), that visitors come to see, and for good reason, as it boasts one of the finest chimneypieces in the world.

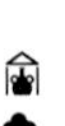

Occupying more than a third of the wall space, this magnificent example of Flemish carving was worked on by various sculptors (1529-31), under the supervision of the Bruges artist Lancelot Blondel. It was commissioned to celebrate the Treaty of Kamerrijk (1529), under which the vassal status of Flanders with the King of France was ended after 600 years. Charles V, Emperor of the Holy Roman Empire and Count of Flanders, had defeated François I at the Battle of Pavia in 1525, and an initial peace treaty was signed at Madrid the following year.

Although some Gothic elements can still be observed, in particular the coats of arms, the figures, which dominate the piece, are undoubt-

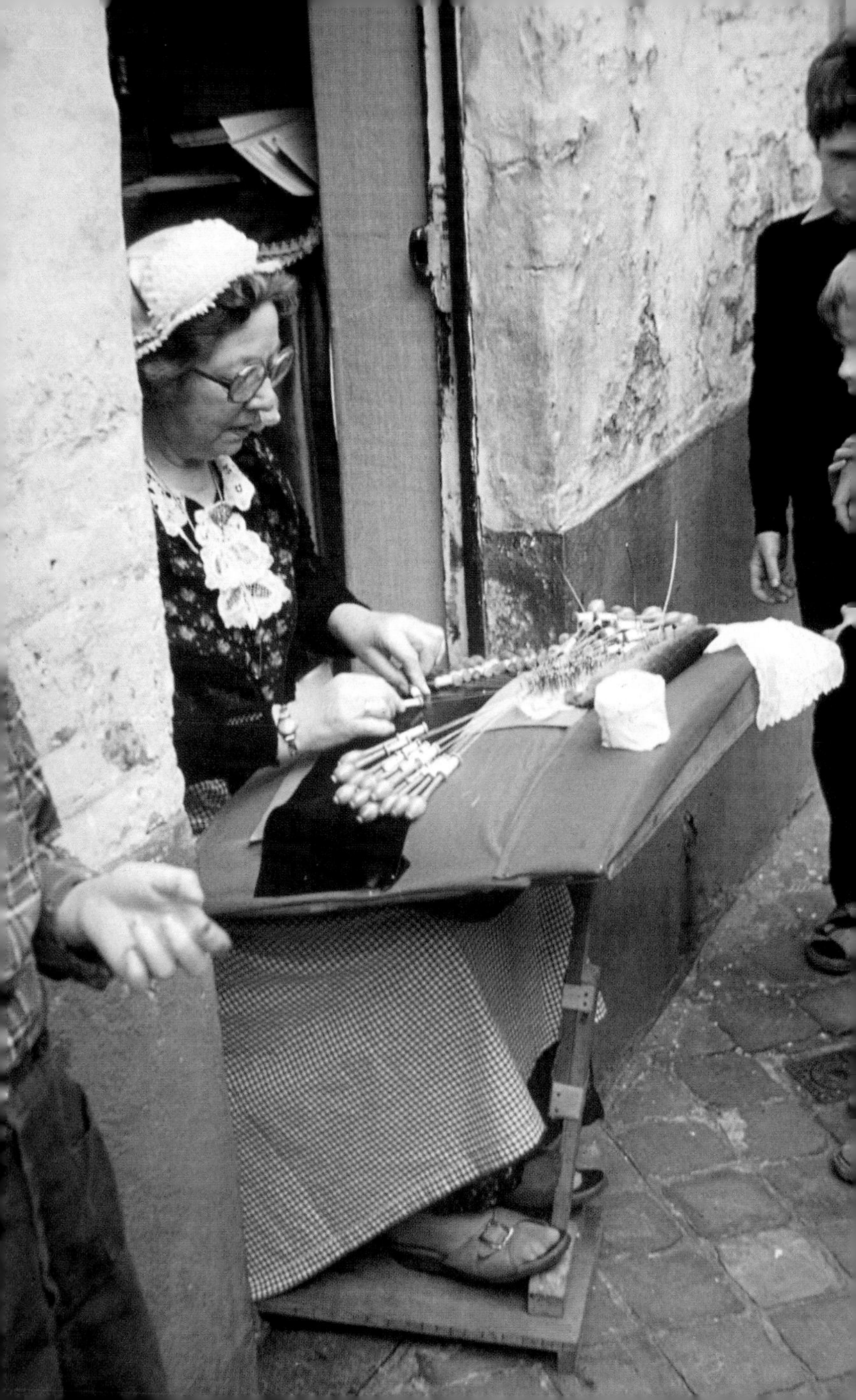

edly Renaissance in style, most of them being carved by Gugot de Beaugrant. Although oak is the prime material employed, black marble and alabaster can also be noted. As may be expected, the main figure is that of Charles V; he is flanked, to the right, by his maternal grandparents Ferdinand and Isabella of Spain and, to the left, by his paternal grandparents Maximilian of Austria (the archduke imprisoned in Craenenburg) and Mary of Burgundy. Behind Charles may just be seen portrait medallions of his parents, Philip the Fair and Joan the Mad (daughter of Ferdinand and Isabella). It would seem that the relegation of his parents to bust representation, together with their part concealment, indicates a wish on the part of Charles to hide them without completely disregarding their existence.

At upper level, even more difficult to identify, are portrait medallions of Charles de Launay, the general who led Charles V's army to victory at Pavia, and the Emperor's aunt, Margaret of Austria, by tradition a prime mover behind the scenes in negotiating the complicated Treaty of Kamerrijk.

Just to show that there were no hard feelings, a portrait medallion of the defeated King of France, François I, is carved to the left of Charles. To the right is a similar bust of the Emperor's sister, Eleanor of Austria, who married François as one of the conditions of the Treaty of Kamerrijk. By such manoeuvering, honour was maintained and loss of face minimised.

The Old Testament story of chaste Susanna is related in the alabaster frieze of the mantelpiece. In the first, while bathing naked, Susanna is surprised by two old men who intend to have their way with her, but she understandably refuses. Infuriated, the men bring charges of adultery against Susanna in court, the penalty for which is death. Daniel, in the third panel, cross examines the men; they are found to be lying, and Susanna is acquitted. In the last panel, the old men are stoned to death.

The Drawing Room, like the Aldermens' Room, added between 1520 and 1525, and the former chapel, added in 1607, now the reading room of the City Archives, are not open to the public.

Sensitively, the citizens of Bruges have disguised their modern shopping developments by planning them in the form of covered multistorey malls set between parallel thoroughfares. Their entrances are kept small, thereby inflicting minimal visual disturbance on the ancient streets. One such development, **Ter Steeghene**, leads from the south-west corner of Burg (just right of the Holy Blood Basilica) to Wollestraat. Steeghene is a reference to the

Facing page: Once a common sight in Bruges, lace makers working outdoors in traditional bonnets now only make rare appearances in the city

staircase linking the two oratories of the Holy Blood Basilica.

At its entrance may be noted **De Sieze**, with an irresistible display of hand-made chocolate pralines; more than fifty different centres are available. Most will wish to move quickly past a rather persistent 'TV cameraman', who offers instant photographs of tourists printed on perpetual calendars; but in general the shops in malls such as Ter Steeghene provide good quality merchandise, avoiding the tattiness found in so many developments of this type in other countries.

At **Wollestraat** (Wool Street), a left turn leads southward in the direction of the city's most important museums.

Located on the main tourist beat, Wollestraat's establishments understandably cater for their needs, with lace, souvenirs, chocolates, ice creams (good and cheap) and fast food restaurants predominating.

Numbering on the east side begins at Markt (odd numbers), but even numbers, on the west side, do not commence until the street called Oude Burg has been passed. This is because the east façade of Halle occupies the entire block. Constructed in 1365, it may be observed that the upper courses of bricks have been completely renewed, eliminating the picturesque battlements, which originally matched those of the existing Markt façade.

A lace shop at **number 9** has been designed in Gothic Revival style; protruding from its façade is an oriel window, behind which a mechanical model of a bonneted lacemaker 'works'. In Bruges until a few years ago many bonneted elderly ladies could be observed sitting outside their doorways making lace in fine weather, but they are now a rare sight. This was not done primarily for the benefit of tourists, but to gain as much natural light as possible so that eye strain would be kept to a minimum. At the time of writing, lacemakers can only usually be seen working outdoors in Walplein, on the second weekend in August.

A short alleyway leads eastward from number 35 Wollestraat, opening up to form a small unnamed square overlooking the canal. Several restaurants take advantage of the idyllic views: **'t Traptje** is recommended for its hearty Flemish casseroles, particularly rabbit simmered in beer.

From 1578 to 1584, the large Gothic house, at **number 53** Wollestraat, accommodated the relic of the Holy Blood. Steps beside the house lead down to one of the many canal boat boarding stages.

On the opposite side of the road, lunettes on the ground floor of 28, a house built in 1634, are decorated with now rather faded polychrome bas-reliefs illustrating the siege of Bruges by Prince Frederik of Nassau's Protestant army in 1613.

De Steen (The Stone), a high, circular tower, was built at the south end of Wollestraat, on the bridge corner, in the eleventh century. This is believed to have served as a residence of the counts of Flanders until Bruges ceased to be their base around 1400. The tower, of the type known as a donjon, then became a prison until fire destroyed most of it in 1689. Only partly restored, all traces of the building were removed in 1785.

Ending Wollestraat is the brick-built **Nepomucenus Bridge**, its name commemorates the Czech St John of Nepomucen, a fourteenth-century Canon of Prague and court chaplain. By tradition, he refused to reveal the confessions of Queen Sophie to her husband, King Wenceslas IV, and was martyred by being thrown in the River Moldau. If the sun is shining, keen photographers may now, rather than later, wish to turn immediately left along **Rozenhoedkaal**, from where the world-famous view of the belfry may be obtained.

In order to reach the museum area, however, it is necessary to follow the canal in the opposite direction, along **Dijver**, a not particularly interesting street of classical houses. Amongst the trees on the canal side there is a flea market Saturdays and Sundays, from 10am-6pm, March to November, when the sedate thoroughfare livens up.

Den Dijver, at number 5, boasts a terrace, where, in summer, snacks and beverages are served; ice creams and pancakes are deservedly popular. Internally, the restaurant is quite delightful: Flemish specialities are given inventive touches.

Europacollege (College of Europe), at 11 Dijver, has been located in Bruges since 1949. In spite of the name, its students come from many countries, their arrival adding a more cosmopolitan and youthful element to the city, which had been greatly needed since the demise of Bruges in the fifteenth century. The college specializes in post-graduate courses, being particularly strong in European-orientated law and economics.

Many will find the **Groeninge Museum** with its world-famous collection of Flemish Primitive paintings, at 12 Groeninge, just about perfect in size and presentation — for once, the visitor leaves a great museum without feeling satiated. This is the only museum of importance in Bruges not to be located in an ancient building. An advantage here is that the structure was designed specifically for the world-famous collection, which it has housed since 1930. It occupies the site of Eekhout Abbey, which was suppressed during the French Revolution and demolished in 1796. The name Groeninge commemorates the plain outside Kortrijk, where the Flemish army defeated the French at the battle of the Golden Spurs in 1302.

All exhibits are captioned in four languages and sympathetically illuminated. Donations and acquisitions have meant that the Groeninge now possesses far more paintings than it has space to exhibit; works, therefore, are periodically rotated, so that all are displayed at some time. Masterly detail and serene expressions vie with macabre scenes of horror that make the nastiest 'video nasty' seem like Mary Poppins in comparison. Glowing colours, with

Flemish Primitives

The Flemish Primitives are definitely not a semi-naked tribe sequestered in a steamy Belgian jungle, but the name coined in the nineteenth century to define the earliest paintings of the Flemish School. No one is quite certain precisely what 'primitive' referred to; it may have meant 'the first', or it could have been an allusion to the artists' ignorance of the use of perspective and accurate proportions. Both the Groeninge and the Memling museums, in Bruges, are internationally renowned for their collections of these great works.

All the Flemish Primitive masters are distinguished by brilliant colours, meticulous, almost childlike attention to detail, and the adoption of landscape backgrounds to give the illusion of depth. It was Philip the Good, Duke of Burgundy (1419-67), who, on transferring his court from Dijon to Bruges, brought with him the finest painters in his dukedom. Pre-eminent among them was Jan van Eyck, whom he employed in 1425 as *peintre at valet de chambre*. Some believe that Van Eyck invented oil painting, although there is no firm evidence for this. It is certain, however, that no other painter of any period has been able to match Van Eyck's technique; his colours remain fresh and brilliant as the day they were first applied. Renowned for the objectivity and deep spirituality of his work, Van Eyck's *Virgin with Canon van der Paele* can be seen in the Groeninge Museum. Not far from Bruges, in Ghent's Sint Baafskathedraal is Van Eyck's masterpiece, the triptych known as *The Adoration of the Mystic Lamb*. The painter died at Bruges in 1441, having lived for many years in his house at Sint Gilliskerkstraat.

Because of the Memling Museum, most visitors to Bruges associate this artist more closely than any other with the city, and he did spend much of his life here, dying in Bruges in 1494. Memling painted primarily religious subjects, but also portraits, being particularly fond of diptychs, one panel of which featured a Madonna and Child and the other the patron, often depicted with his or her patron saint. These could be folded and were therefore easy to transport; few now remain in their double-panel state. Memling was the most prolific of all the Flemish Primitives, but some have noted an insipid quality in his paintings, in spite of their technical brilliance. The painter's most famous work, the *Shrine of St Ursula*, is displayed in the Memling Museum.

Hugo van der Goes (c1440-1482), may have been born in Bruges but this is uncertain. At the age of 27 he was accepted as a master in the Painter's Guild of Ghent, where he gained many commissions. Charles the Bold certainly held Van der Goes in high esteem, as he placed him in charge of the decoration of Bruges to celebrate his marriage. In 1475, Van der Goes entered a convent near Brussels; he is believed to have become mentally unstable and even, so it is said, attempted suicide. His work was certainly disturbing, as will be noted in the Groeninge Museum's *Death of the Virgin*, completed shortly before his own demise. The bright colours are unreal, and, combined with the grieving expressions of the Disciples, create a sense of unease. It is considered that the masterpiece of Van der Goes is his *Portinari* triptych, commissioned by the Medici representation in Bruges. It is, in fact, the only fully documented work by the artist, and can be seen in the Uffizi, Florence.

Petrus Christus (1415-1472), who was working in Bruges 3 years after the death of Van Eyck, painted in a similar style to the master. One panel of a triptych, *Isabella of Portugal* (possibly) with Saint Elizabeth, is in the Groeninge collection.

Gerard David (c1460-1523), came to Bruges from what is now Holland, and lived many years in the city. His gruesome diptych, *The Judgement of Cambyses,* commissioned in 1498 for the Stadhuis in Burg, is a major attraction at the Groeninge Museum, although his *Baptism of Christ* triptych, usually in the same gallery, is considered by many to be a finer work.

Dirk Bouts (1415-75) was the first Flemish painter to adopt Renaissance techniques for creating an illusion of depth through single point perspective and the accurate proportioning of figures to other objects. Perhaps he should not really be defined as a Primitive.

The end of the Burgundian dukedom coincided with the decline of Bruges, and the two events heralded a slow decline in the quality of Flemish painting. In the sixteenth century, only Hieronymus Bosch (1450-1516), and Pieter Breughel (1529-69), both, in effect, early Surrealists, can be regarded as Flemish masters of great importance. More than a century was to pass before the Baroque works of the Antwerp School, led by Rubens and Van Dyck would restore greatness to Flemish painting.

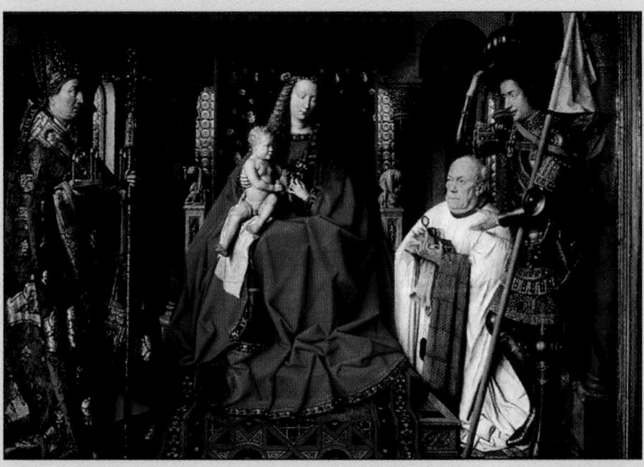

Undoubtedly the greatest painting in Bruges is the Van Eyck altarpiece of the *Madonna with Canon van der Paele.* Its colours are as fresh as when they were painted almost 500 years ago no sign of cracks, emphasise that the techniques of the Flemish Primitives were in no way primitive. It is hard to believe that most paintings on display are more than 500 years old.

Always exhibited are two paintings by Van Eyck: *a portrait of the painter's wife, Margareta,* and the *Madonna with Canon van der Paele* altarpiece. Margareta was 33 years old when painted by her husband; such portraits were rare at the time, when almost all paintings had religious themes. By the look of the sitter, however, it would have been a brave man who refused to paint her if she wanted him to! The Van de Paele altarpiece was commissioned for the donor's private chapel in Sint Donaas Cathedral. St George and St Donaas are depicted on the right.

Not to be missed is the anonymous *portrait of Lodewijk van Gruuthuse,* whose mansion now forms the Gruuthuse Museum. On his chain he wears the emblem of the Order of the Golden Fleece.

The *Martyrdom of St Hippolytus* is an important triptych by Derk Bouts and Hugo Van der Goes, whilst Death of the Virgin is entirely the work of Van der Goes.

Memling's *Moreel triptych* is this artists most important work at the Groeninge; six further masterpieces by this painter are displayed in the Memling Museum.

Those of a nervous disposition should visit room 6 with some trepidation, particularly on approaching the double-panelled *Judgement of Cambyses,* by Gerard David, commissioned for the Aldermens Room at Stadhuis in 1498. Cambyses, a Persian king, orders the arrest of a judge accused of corruption, and he is found guilty in the first panel. In the second, the King's sentence is carried out — flaying alive. Stretched out on a table, while his body is expertly skinned, the face of the guilty judge is supposed to be modelled on that of Pieter Lanchals, executed in Bruges 10 years earlier. A rather more severe work by the same painter, *Baptism of Christ,* hangs in the gallery.

Perhaps most gruesome of all is the *Last Judgement,* by Hieronymus Bosch, a Surrealist nightmare of demons and goblins, designed to impress that hell was not the best of places in which to spend eternity.

The Kantmuseum (Lace Museum) and the Brangwyn Museum occupy separate floors of the same eighteenth-century mansion, which straddles the canal at 16 Dijver. Presumably for reasons of administrative convenience, the price of admission covers both museums.

Located on the ground floor, the **Lace Museum** is based on the collection donated by Baroness Liedts. The evolution of 'Van Dijck' bobbin lace from the seventeenth century is demonstrated. Exhibits include needlepoint work from France and Italy in addition to Flanders. It will be noted that with age lace gradually becomes cream in colour, a helpful, but not necessarily infallible sign of authenticity. Most will be impressed by the copy of a full-length painting of Empress Maria Theresa dressed in

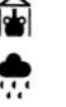

Brussels lace, the work of the Bruges artist Matthias de Visch, dating from around 1750.

A staircase gives access from the hall to the **Brangwyn Museum**. Frank Brangwyn was born at Bruges in 1867, but his Welsh father, William Brangwyn, took the family to England when the boy was only 10 years old. Nevertheless, Frank Brangwyn obviously retained a great affection for the city of his birth, and presented this collection of his work to Bruges in 1936 'as a memorial of my love for your great city'.

Brangwyn is best known for his romantic oil paintings, which, at their best, can be reminiscent of Delacroix, with their brilliant colours and sinuous forms. At Bruges, however, most of the work displayed is graphic, etchings of the Begijnhof and Van Eyckplein bearing witness to Brangwyn's return visits to Bruges. The artist was certainly influenced by contemporary trends, noteworthy being the Art Nouveau character of some of his ex libris designs and the carpet, *De Wingerd* (Vineyard), of 1897. Examples of wooden furniture designed by Brangwyn are displayed throughout the galleries, most of them being Art Deco in style.

Two large oil paintings, *Slave Market* and an allegorical *British Empire* are perhaps the most important works on display. The latter was one of a set commissioned for the Royal Gallery of the House of Lords, Westminster, by Lord Iveagh, and painted between 1925 and 1930. Hung experimentally in the House of Lords for a short time, the works were eventually rejected as being 'too modern' for the building. Late-nineteenth-century watercolours of Tangier and Egypt are valuable topographical records in addition to being examples of Brangwyn's skill in that medium. Frank Brangwynd died at Ditchling, Sussex, in 1956.

Opposite the entrance to the museums, and visible through large windows, is a collection of ancient coaches and sledges.

A pathway leads southward from the museum to **Arentspark**, formerly the grounds of the Gruuthuse mansion, which is located on the opposite side of the canal. In the park have been erected two stone columns from the thirteenth-century Waterhalle, which stood on the east side of Markt until demolished in 1787. Facing them are bronze equestrian figures representing the Knights of the Apocalypse: death, war, famine and revolution, the work of sculptor Rik Poot, 1987. From the west bank of the park there is an attractive view over the canal to the Gruuthuse courtyard.

Crossing the waterway to Gruuthuse and Onze-Lieve-Vrouwekerk is **Bonifacius Bridge**, one of the most picturesque in Bruges, although the present hump-backed structure only dates from 1910. Seen from the bridge, looking back to the small building attached to it, is a venerable waterside inn sign of stone, carved with a boat; it was brought here from Nieuwpoort. Exceptional views of the chancel of Onze-Lieve-Vrouwekerk are gained from here.

Immediately left of the bridge, on

Lace

It will be impossible to miss the lace shops in Bruges, and many will also wish to visit the Lace Museum and the Lace Centre, where the skilful lace makers can be observed at work. Although a primitive type of lace has been found in Ancient Egyptian tomb chambers, lace in its modern form was a European invention. The chief difference between lace and embroidery, which it resembles, is that lace is an ornamental fabric in itself, not an addition to one that already exists. There are two basic techniques — needlepoint, which is extremely difficult, and was probably invented in Italy in the fifteenth century, and bobbin lace, which also involves great skill in its more elaborate forms. On occasion, needlepoint and bobbin methods are combined.

Until 1800, the thread used in lace making was almost always linen, although silk, metal and even fine wool were occasionally employed. After 1800, however, cotton thread began to be used more extensively than linen due to its lower cost — but the results were never quite as spectacular.

Bobbin lace probably evolved in Flanders in the early sixteenth century, to cope with the demand for lace trim to both men's and women's clothing. Late fifteenth-century Italian and Flemish portraits show hems and seams trimmed with lace, and by 1600 the lace industry was of great importance in western Europe. France, particularly north-west France, in addition to Flanders and Italy, was a large producer, and lace was also made commercially in Spain, Germany and England, where Nottingham lace, in particular, gained an enviable reputation.

By the nineteenth century, lace had fallen completely out of fashion with men, and even women were wearing little of it. All was to change around 1840, however, when fashion did a complete turnabout, and lace was once again in vogue — but for women's fashions only. Mechanical methods were introduced, cotton completely replaced linen thread, and the design standards fell. It was not until 1920 that lace would disappear from the fashion scene, but this time its demise in this market would appear to be final, with the exception of trim for ladies underwear. Lace is still made in Europe, particularly Bruges and Burano, Italy, now primarily for souvenirs such as doylies, and trim for linen articles. China, Taiwan and South-East Asia are also producers.

The first lace making school in Bruges was founded by three nuns from Antwerp, but not until the early years of the eighteenth century. There was so little employment in Bruges at the time that lace making soon became a popular means by which poor women could earn a living. Prices paid by the merchants were not high, however fine the work, and many toiled for too many hours in order to make a living. In consequence, their eyesight suffered, and many an elderly lacemaker became partially or even completely blind. It was not long before the inventions of the Industrial Revolution were to be applied to lace making, and handmade bobbin lace then became no more than a part-time activity.

Only tourist demand has preserved the lace industry in Bruges; the skills of the ladies who make it are demonstrated at the Lace Centre in Peperstraat, where items are for sale, but elsewhere, purchasers of lace in Bruges must beware factory-made imports from South-East Asia. Typical Bruges 'Duchesse' lace, produced from either thin or thick thread, employs delicate floral designs. Up to 200 bobbins are employed in Point de Fee, the most exquisite of all Bruges lace. Genuine Bruges lace must display a Quality Control label: the Tourist Office will provide a list of outlets where the lace is guaranteed to be genuine.

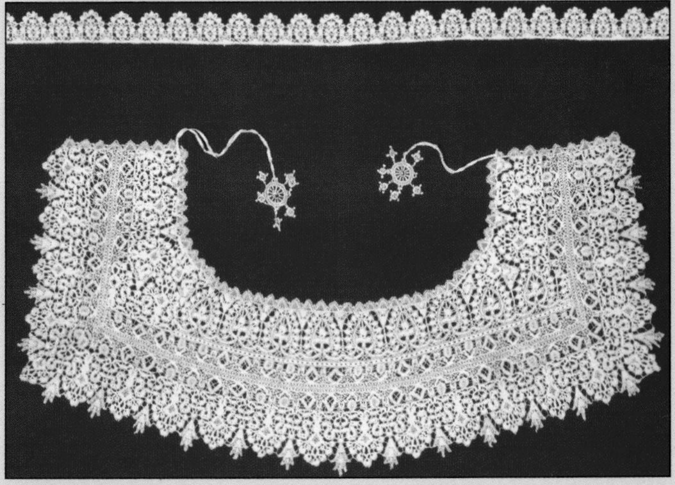

Bruges (and non-Bruges) lace is sold from many shops in Bruges. Once an important industry, lace making would almost certainly have died out in the city were it not for tourist interest

the opposite bank of the canal, is a **bust of Joan Luis Vives** (1492-1540), a Catalan from Valencia, who lived many years in Bruges, where he met fellow humanists Erasmus and Sir Thomas More. Vives worked strenuously to relieve the condition of the poor in Flanders.

Immediately right, after the bridge has been crossed, rises the bare brick rear wall of the Gruuthuse mansion, bare that is apart from an exquisite little Gothic double window, dating from around 1470. The street leading to the Gruuthuse mansion branches right, whereas that branching left, Onze-Lieve-Vrouwe-Kerkhof Zuid, is more convenient for entering the church, the most important in Bruges, and where Michelangelo's *Virgin and Child* sculpture may be seen. It should be remembered, however, that rather indulgently, the building is closed between 11.30am and 2.30pm.

On route to the church, two houses, at **numbers 6 and 8**, are splendid examples of Art Nouveau work, built around 1904. Although Europe's finest architectural examples of this style, which is also known as Jugendstil (German), are to be found in Brussels, little was built in Bruges.

For many, **Onze-Lieve-Vrouwekerk** (Church of Our Lady), often understandably abbreviated to O-L-V, will be the first church visited in Bruges. Due to the absence of stone quarries in the vicinity, all were built of brick which, in fact, weathers better than stone. It does, of course, preclude carving, and external decoration is usually restricted to ribs of brick curved to form Gothic tracery and to add delicacy or apparent height to the structures. The present church was begun in the thirteenth century and completed in the fifteenth century. Much of its design, particularly that of the chancel and west towers, is reminiscent of Tournai Cathedral, the early-Gothic style of which was itself influenced by the great structures of northern France. Two earlier churches, both Romanesque, had previously occupied the site, the first of which is believed to have dated from the ninth century.

The great spire of the church is 122m (400ft) high, and would still be the world's highest structure of brick masonry if Antwerp Cathedral's spire had not eclipsed it by just 1m (3ft) in 1518 — perhaps someone at Antwerp had a divine revelation that the *Guinness Book of Records* would eventually make an appearance! Work began on the spire in the thirteenth century, and was completed by 1350; the present top section, however, is a fifteenth-century addition. In 1465, a late-Gothic portal of white stone was added to the north side of the tower. Known as Paradijsportaal (Gateway to Paradise), it is no longer an entrance, but has been fitted to serve as an oratory chapel, and has been used as a baptistery.

Onze-Lieve-Vrouwekerk is nowadays entered from the south portal. It is interesting to note in the nave that the triforium arcade is round-headed in Romanesque style, while above this, the slightly larger clerestory windows are pointed, in the

Gothic manner, possibly a measure of the construction progress, as taste changed. The nave's most noteable furnishing is its Baroque eighteenth-century pulpit.

Most will now make for the south aisle, at the east end of which, set within a niche of black marble, is the *Virgin and Child* by Michelangelo (1475-1564), sculpted in contrasting white marble. For reasons of security, it is not permitted to approach the masterpiece too closely, and only those with binoculars will be able to fully appreciate the serenity of the Virgin's expression. A balustrade is conveniently placed on which cameras may be rested, thus avoiding the necessity for fast film, flash or a tripod in order to take successful photographs of the work when the light is reasonable.

The carving was commissioned by Sienna Cathedral in Tuscany, but its funds had run out by the time the work was finished, in 1505, and a Brugean merchant of Italian descent, Jan Moscroen, was able to purchase the sculpture the following year. In 1514, the city treasurer of Bruges, with the financial assistance of wealthy merchants, presented the piece to the church, where it has remained almost ever since. The only exceptions were an expedition to Paris during the French Revolution and another to Germany in World War II, during which, no doubt, it gave much pleasure to that well-known procuror of the arts, Hermann Goering. This is believed to be the only piece of work by Michelangelo that left Italy during his lifetime. The figure was almost contemporary with the same artist's famous Pietà, now at St Peter's, in the Vatican, and demonstrates a similar delicacy, typical of Michelangelo's early work.

A charge is made for entering the chancel and its ambulatory (from the south side); admission is permitted from 10am, but by 11.30am, after 90 minutes work, the exhausted attendants close the area, together with the rest of the church as has already been noted. All comes to life again, however, at 2.30pm, when admission is granted for another 2 hours.

In 1468, the eleventh Chapter of the Order of the Golden Fleece was convened in the chancel to celebrate the third marriage of Charles the Bold, Duke of Burgundy, this time with Margaret of York, sister of England's King Edward IV, who had become a close and grateful friend. The fifteenth-century coats of arms of the knights attending the ceremony have survived, that of Edward IV being above the front stall on the north side; the stalls themselves date from the eighteenth century.

In front of the high altar is a triptych *Passion*, mostly painted between 1534 and 1561 by Bernard van Orley of Brussels, although completed by Marcus Gerards.

Behind the altar are the gilded tombchests of Charles the Bold and

---

Following page: Bonifacius Bridge links the Brangwyn Museum with Onze Lieve Vrouwekerk and the Gruuthuse Museum

---

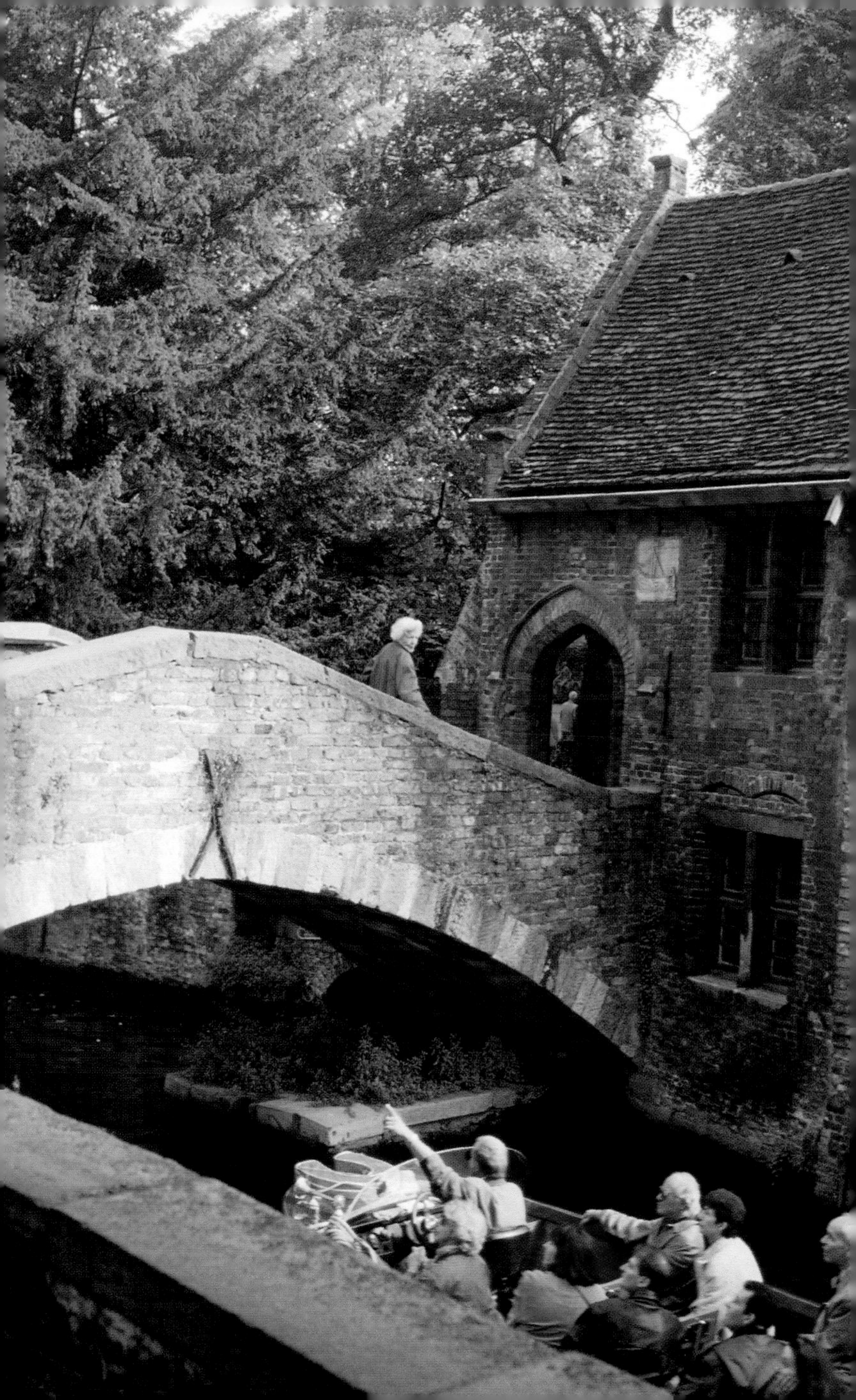

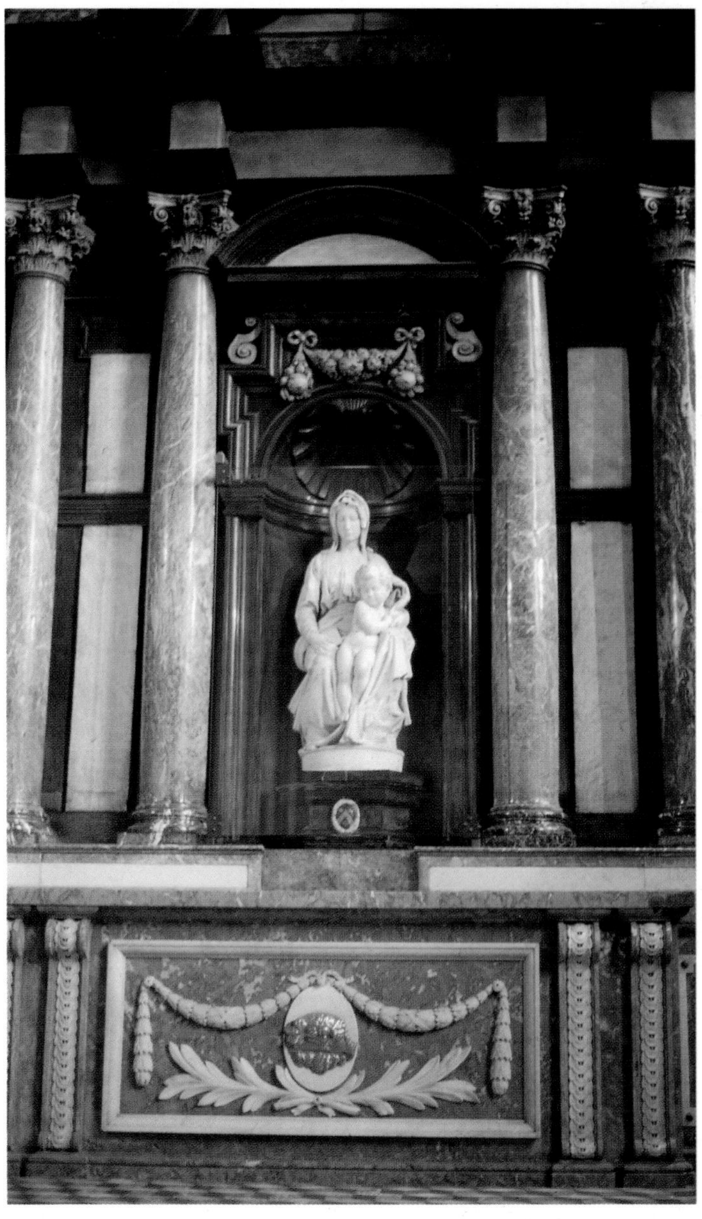

his daughter, Mary of Burgundy. Although Mary died in 1482, 5 years after her father her tomb was made earlier. She met her death, aged 24, falling from a horse whilst hunting with falcons. Archduke Maximilian of Austria, her husband, grieved 'Never, as long as I live, will I forget this faithful woman.' The recumbent tomb figure of Margaret was cast by Renier van Thienen, and gilded by a Bruges jeweller.

The tombchest of Charles the Bold lies beside that of his daughter, on which its design is modelled. Charles was killed during the siege of Nancy in 1477, but it was several days before what was believed to be his mutilated body was discovered in a frozen pond, and interred at Nancy. Eighty-three years later, Charles V ordered that his great grandfather's remains should be transferred to Bruges, but by the time they arrived — after a mysterious three-year sojourn in Luxembourg — Charles V had abdicated. It was left to his son and successor, Philip II, to commission a suitable tomb, which was designed by Jacob Jonghelinck of Antwerp. Charles the Bold's slogan, which may be translated as 'I have made the venture, may it prosper', is inscribed on the tomb. His recumbent figure is similar in style to that of Mary.

Between the tombchests and the altar, visible below ground through glass, are examples of thirteenth- and fourteenth-century open tombs, their inner sides painted with religious themes in a manner that calls to mind the post-death considerations of the Ancient Egyptians. All were discovered in 1979.

Against the wall of the ambulatory's Lanchals chapel stands the black tombchest of Pieter Lanchals, decorated on its face with his swan emblem; *lanchals* in Dutch means longneck, and the emblem was, therefore, a pun, a common practise at the time. Lanchals was executed at Markt in 1488 for 'treacherously' supporting Maximilian of Austria's tax increases on the Bruges citizens. By tradition, the introduction of swans to the city's canals was ordered so that Brugeans would be constantly reminded of their mistreatment of Lanchals. A municipal official, in addition to advising Maximilian, Lanchals resided in a large house in Oude Burg, part of which still exists.

In 1472, Lodewijk van Gruuthuse built a lower and an upper chapel for the exclusive use of his family. The lower chapel, now closed, provided direct entrance to the north ambulatory, while even greater privacy could be obtained from the oratory above, as it was linked, via a bridge over O.L.V. Kerkhof Noord, with his mansion. Plus est en vous (More is in you), inscribed on the chapel, was the motto of Lodewijk, apparently a reference to the exhortation that he

Preceding page: Michelangelo's serene *Virgin and Child* occupies a niche in Onze-Lieve-Vrouwekerk — a Renaissance masterpiece in a Baroque city

gave his troops in battle. Although only the oriel window of the chapel may be glimpsed from the north ambulatory of the church, visitors to the Gruuthuse Museum are able to enter it.

After leaving the church, turn right into Gruuthusestraat, which fronts the museum. Before entering the courtyard it is as well to admire the stone frieze depicting battle scenes, which decorates the external wall of the outhouse. This is genuine fifteenth-century carving, unlike most of the other architectural features of Gruuthuse, which are nineteenth-century pastiche Gothic, the over-enthusiastic work of restorer Louis Delacenserie.

The courtyard of the **Gruuthuse Museum** may be entered free of charge. Right of the entrance is the former stable block, now a tearoom.

Eventually, Gruuthuse became the L-shaped mansion which is now seen, but it evolved from the two-storey step-gabled house on the right. This was built by Jan van Gruuthuse in 1425, who fixed the coat of arms of himself and his wife to the gable. The two identical Gothic balustrades of stone above the first floor windows are original.

Jan's son Lodewijk added the bridging oratory chapel to his father's house in 1472, but prior to this (1465-70), he had greatly extended the original building by the addition of two further ranges, forming the present L shape.

The Gruuthuse family's name, in addition to its wealth, came from *gruut*, the Dutch word for grout, a secret combination of dried plants used by brewers to flavour beer before the introduction of hops. In the thirteenth century, the family was granted the right to levy a duty on all grout used by the brewers of Bruges, and they changed their name from Van Brugghe-van der Aa to Gruuthuse.

Lodewijk van Gruuthuse became one of the wealthiest and most important men in the Netherlands; his inumerable titles, awarded by Charles the Bold, whose marriage with Mary of Burgundy he had helped arrange, included: Knight of the Order of the Golden Fleece, Governor of Holland, Zeeland and West Friesland, and Commander of the Burgundian military forces. Lodewijk developed a close relationship with King Edward IV, supporting him financially in his successful efforts to regain the throne of England in the final stage of the Wars of the Roses. During his brief exile from England, Edward stayed at Gruuthuse from October 1470 to April 1471, accompanied by his apparently faithful brother Richard. This was the man who would later be crowned King Richard III, and later still branded by William Shakespeare and the majority of historians as the monster who murdered his brother Edward's two young sons in the Tower of London.

Following page: The courtyard of the Gruuthuse Museum seen from Arentspark, which was formerly its garden

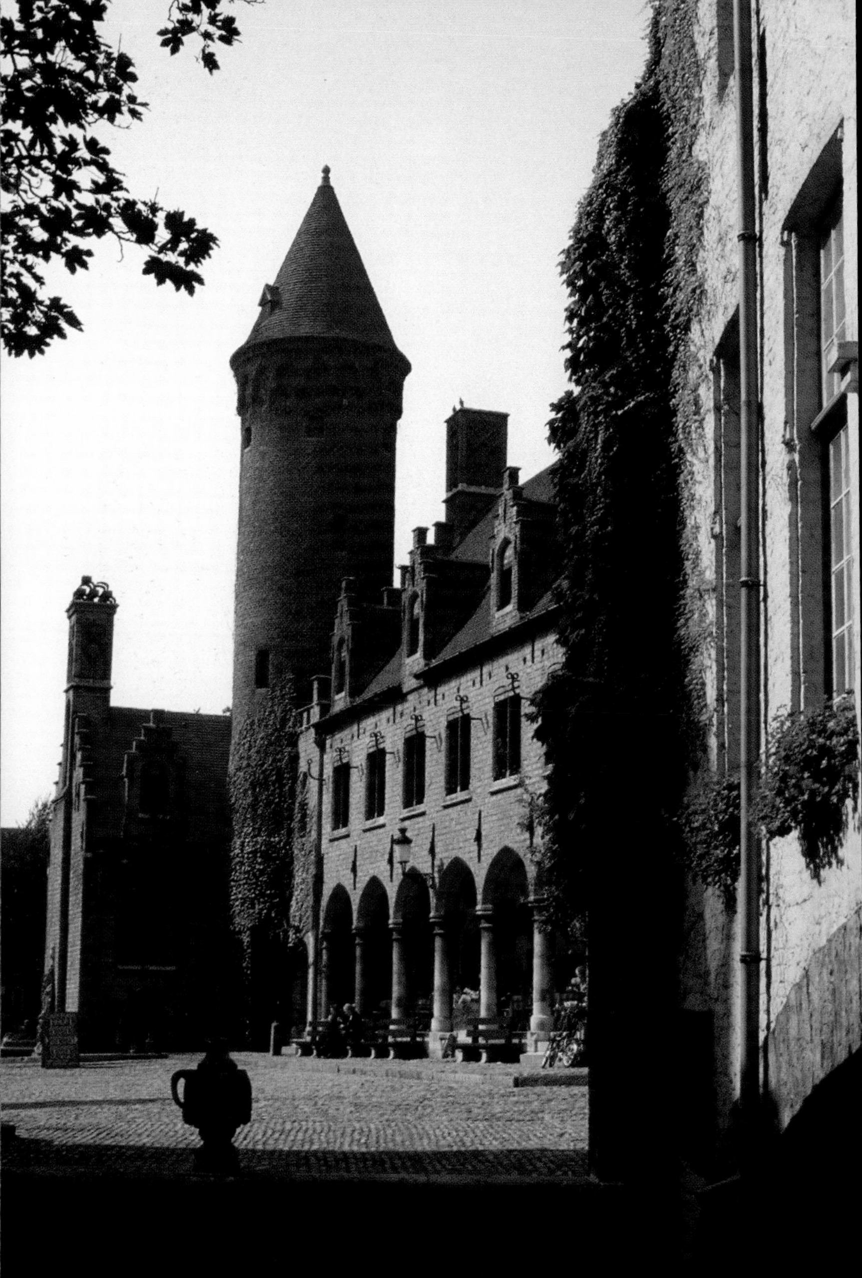

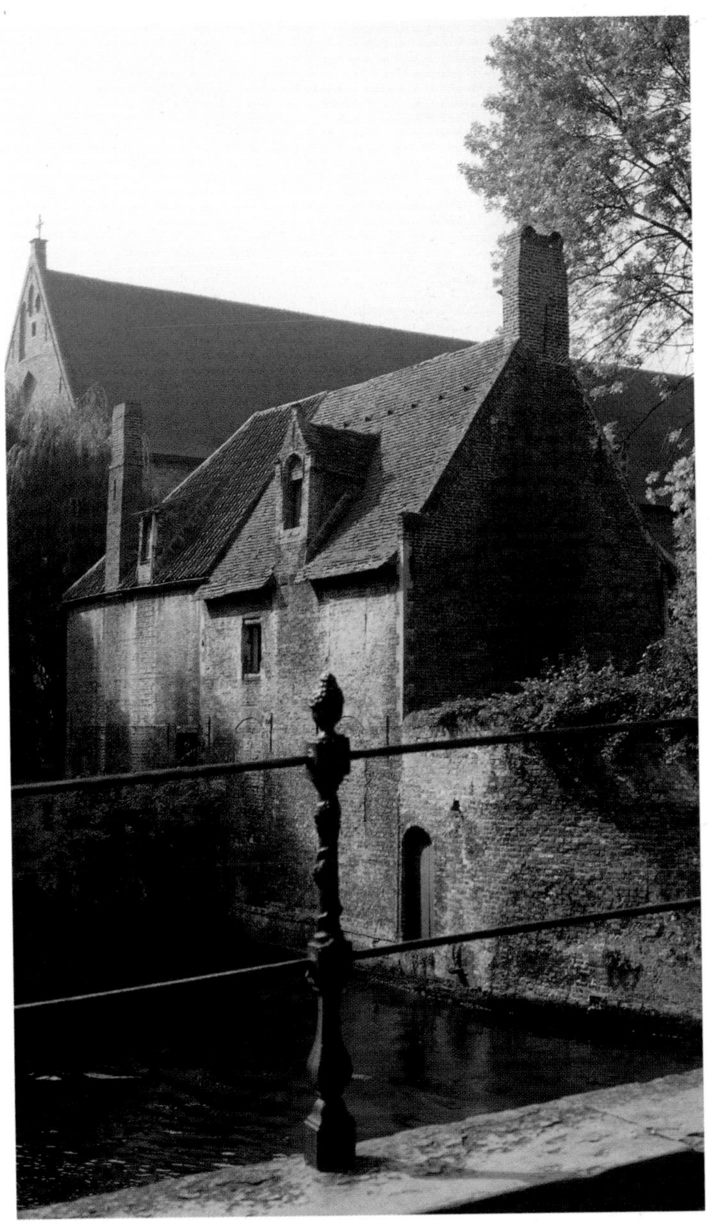

As a reward for Lodewijk's assistance, Edward appointed him Earl of Winchester on regaining his throne. When Lodewijk, a patron of the arts, died in 1492, he had ammassed an exceptional collection of illustrated manuscripts, but his son, who allied himself with France, left Bruges for Abbeville and sold the collection, which now forms part of the archives of the Bibliothèque Nationale in Paris.

By the sixteenth century, Bruges had become an unfashionable address, well into its 'Rip Van Winkel' period, and Gruuthuse remained empty until 1628, when a charitable lending bank, Mons Pietas, took over the premises. Banks charging low interest rates, sometimes none at all, had been founded in Italy to break the monopoly of the Lombards, whose rates were extortionate, and similar establishments were set up in Flanders by Archduchess Isabella. The Dutch word *Mons* (Mountain) was a mistranslation of the Italian *Monte* (Money).

By the nineteenth century, the Gruuthuse mansion had become a dilapidated pawnbroker's store; it was rescued by being chosen as the venue for the collection of Flemish antiques put together by local enthusiasts that included British exiles William Brangwyn and John Steinmetz. Louis Delacensier was given the task of converting the house to a museum, which he began in 1892. It seems that apart from the kitchen and the oratory chapel, most original Gothic features had already been lost, and the architect added his own Gothic Revival work, a common late-nineteenth-century solution throughout northern Europe. Apart from the two rooms mentioned, therefore, the picturesque fireplaces, balustrades and carvings throughout are relatively modern work.

The varied collection of antiques displayed throughout Gruuthuse includes musical instruments, furniture, altarpieces, ceramics and coins. Unfortunately, in spite of a not inconsiderable entrance fee, captions, with the sole, risible exception of 'Do not touch', are written exclusively in Dutch, a language comprehended by few tourists. They are also faded, and many of them located where they cannot be read by anyone: the situation, it must be said, is reminiscent of a museum in a third world country. Apparently, a multi-language description of the exhibits has been in preparation for 5 years, but at the time of writing there is no sign of its completion. Look out for the famous painted bust of Charles V (*Buste van Keizer Karel I*) in **room 1**. It was made of terracotta in 1520 and decorated later.

In **room 3** is an amusing painting of a baby being washed; it would appear that the procedure included giving the poor infant an enema, and an appliance of the type used in the scene, resembling a bicycle pump, is exhibited below the picture.

Preceding page: Protected by its high wall, the Begijnhof from outside resembles a separate, fortified village

Most impressive, however, is the great kitchen and, on the upper floor, **room 16a**, the oratory (*Bidkapel of Oratorium*) added by Lodewijk van Gruuthuse to his father's house. From its window can be seen the sanctuary of Onze-Lieve-Vrouwekerk. An enchanting view of Bonifacius Bridge is gained from the loggia outside **room 21**.

Facing the entrance to the Gruuthuse Museum is **Guido Gezelleplein**, named to commemorate the most famous Flemish poet, a priest, who lived from 1830 to 1899. His statue, erected in 1930 to commemorate the centenary of his birth, is the work of Jules Lagre. The birthplace of Guido Geselle, now a museum, may be visited in north Bruges.

Gruuthusestraat continues westward, joining Mariastraat, left, where, on the west side, at **number 38**, a range of ancient buildings form Sint Janshospitaal, within which the Memling Museum is located.

Founded as a monastic establishment, around 1150, on the west bank of the river, which then marked the eastern boundary of Bruges, **Sint Janshospitaal** (St John's Hospital) is one of Europe's most ancient hospices, and was still operating as an infirmary in the nineteenth century. Only fragments of the original structure have survived. Housed within the former chapel is the **Memling Museum**.

Five linked but distinct structures form the **Mariastraat** façade; from right to left these are: a ward with an entrance archway, circa 1290; an early thirteenth-century tower with Romanesque windows; the hospital chapel, built in Gothic style between the late-thirteenth and early-fourteenth centuries; a Romanesque ward, early thirteenth century, but with a Gothic portal added later in the same century, its tympanum carved both externally and internally to depict the *Death and Coronation of the Virgin*; finally comes the Gothic ward, built in 1315.

The complex is entered through the archway. Immediately right, approached from a cloister passageway, the seventeenth-century **pharmacy** of the hospital only ceased to be used in 1976. Items such as bottles, wooden dressers and splendid examples of Delftware jars are seen, many in their original position. In the rear room, a cupboard is carved with a bas-relief depicting a hospital ward, in which patients can be seen two to a bed: one trusts that modern welfare state economies will not have to repeat such drastic measures! Not only the sick, but impecunious travellers were accommodated in the hospital, many of whom would have been used to sharing a bed with a stranger. The hospital possesses an even better record of the ward's appearance, revealed in an eighteenth-century painting by

Following page: Grouped around a green, most houses in the Begijnhof date from the seventeenth and eighteenth centuries, although they remain medieval in style

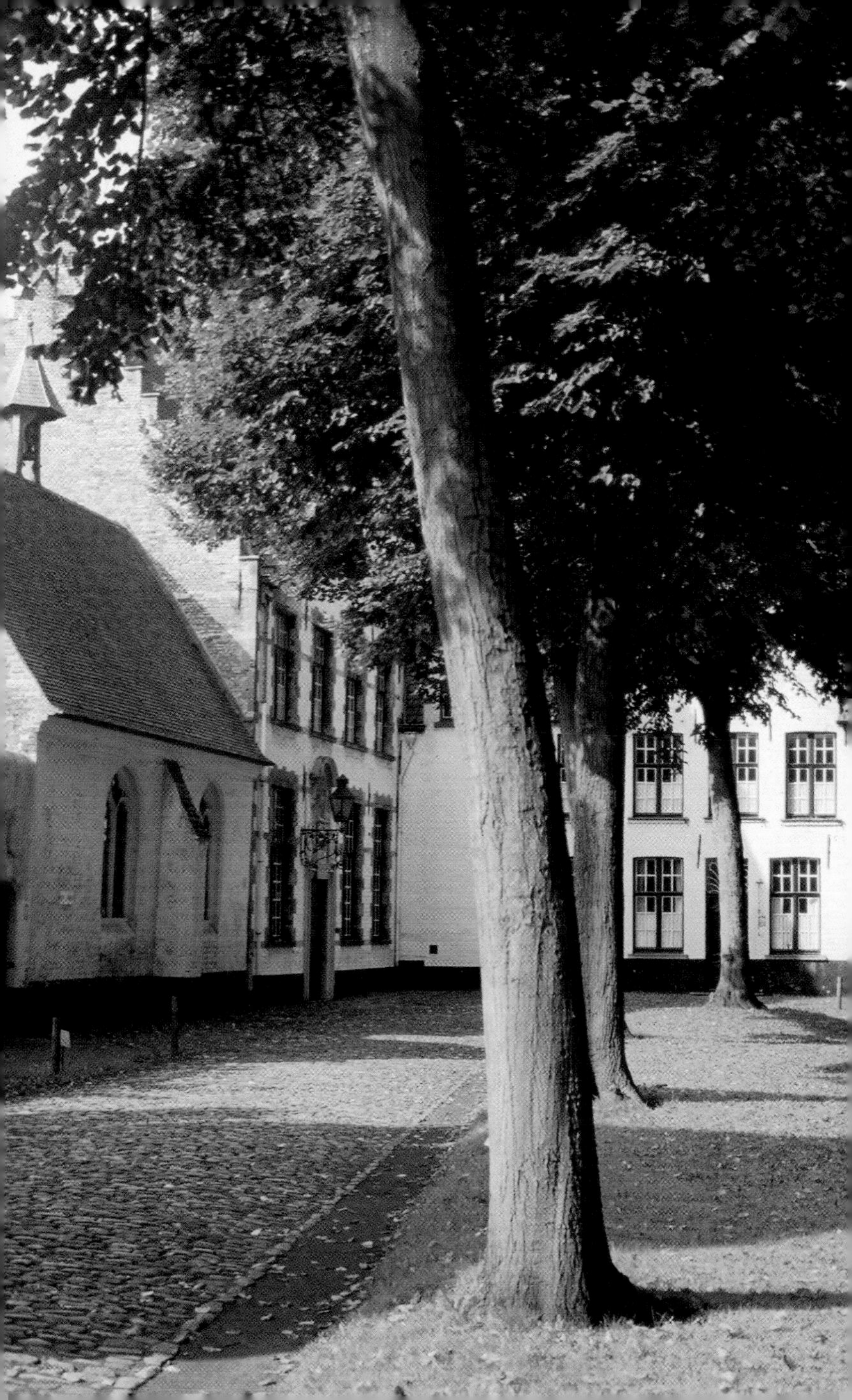

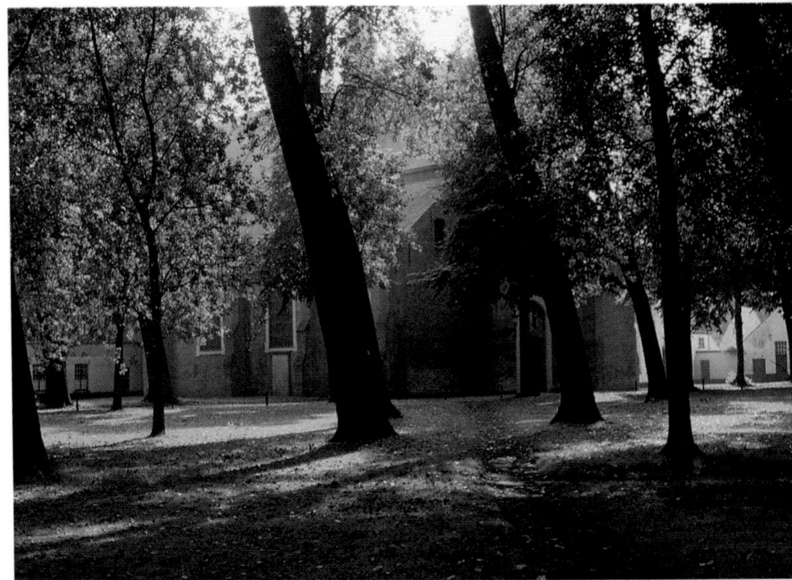

The Begijnhof church, dedicated to St Elizabeth of Hungary, was rebuilt in the early seventeenth century

Jan Beerblock. Beds are created in alcoves, patients are transported on wooden litters and dogs perambulate.

Entry tickets are obtained on the opposite side of the entrance, just after the archway has been passed. At the time of writing, restoration of the ancient wards to their original form was in progress, and visitors could not be admitted to them. It is not expected that they will be reopened before late 1997 at the earliest. The hospital's outstanding collection of Memling paintings, accommodated in the former chapel of the hospital, are fortunately unaffected.

On entering the former **chapel** it should be born in mind that the blocked archways of the south wall were originally open to the adjoining ward; dying or very sick patients could therefore celebrate Mass without leaving their beds.

Displayed in the nave are the four works commissioned from Memling for the hospital. Hans Memling was born some time between 1435 and 1440, at Seligenstadt, a prosperous town near Frankfurt. He is known to have been in residence at Bruges and reasonably affluent by 1465. Bruges was then at the height of its importance, and the young painter received many commissions from wealthy merchants and diplomats visiting the city; for this reason, his works are distributed widely amongst European collections. Eventually Memling must have amassed quite a fortune for the time, as he is known to have owned three houses in the city. He died at Bruges in 1494.

First seen is the world-famous *Shrine of St Ursula*. This was made to contain relics of the saint in the possession of the hospital, and commissioned by two of its sisters around 1480. Made of gilded wood, the reliquary is entirely Gothic in style. In one of the painted panels can be seen the two sisters who commissioned the work kneeling before the Virgin Mary. Like so many religious legends, that of St Ursula dates from the thirteenth century. Believed to be a princess from Brittany, Ursula consented to marry a pagan king if he converted to Christianity and sent her, accompanied by other virgins, on a pilgrimage to Rome to receive the Pope's blessing. On their return journey, the virgins were captured in Cologne by Huns, who demanded that they should renounce Christianity; they refused and were put to death. In the paintings that relate the tale, St Ursula is depicted wearing blue and white garments, similar to those that frequently identify the Virgin Mary. Particularly valuable topographically are Memling's views of medieval Cologne, a city that he knew well.

Centrally placed in front of the altar is the large *St John the Baptist* and *St John the Evangelist* triptych, painted specifically for the high altar of the hospital's church in 1479. It is generally referred to as the St John altarpiece, but occasionally as the Mystic Marriage of St Catherine, due to the central panel in which the infant Christ is depicted presenting St Catherine with a ring. It has been suggested that Memling modelled his portrait of the saint on Mary of Burgundy. Also featured are St John the Baptist and St John the Evangelist, patron saints of the hospital; the fronts of the side panels illustrate scenes from their lives, whilst the backs depict the four donors of the triptych kneeling before their patron saints.

Displayed against the south wall of the nave is a much smaller triptych, commissioned for the hospital by another of its brothers, Jan Floreins, in 1479, and known as the *Adoration of the Magi* triptych. The 36 year-old-Floreins is shown kneeling to the left of the central panel. Left of the Virgin, the king may be a portrait of Charles the Bold; some also think that Memling depicted himself looking from the window right, sporting the yellow headwear worn by patients of Sint Janshospitaal. Yet a third, but less impressive triptych, *Lamentations over Christ*, is seen next. It was commissioned from Memling the following year by another brother of the hospital, Adriaan Reins, and is based on a work by Rogier van der Weyden, at whose studio in Brussels Memling had learnt his craft before coming to Bruges. Here, the donor kneels in the left panel. In spite of its emotional subject, the central panel fails to move. Painted on the right panel is an appealing St Barbara.

Against the wall of the north

chapel are two works transferred here from the St Juliaanshospitaal in south Bruges, which closed in 1815. The first is a mysterious portrait, believed by some to be the daughter of Willem Moreel, Burgemaster of Bruges in 1480, when the work was painted. Inscribed at the top left corner of the Renaissance-period frame of the painting is the name Sibylla Sambetha; below is quoted the Persian Sybil's prophecy of Christ's coming. It is not known who was responsible for this or why the title was chosen, but the name has stuck, the portrait being generally known as *Sibylla Sambetha*; it is probably just the ethereal expression of the young lady that is responsible.

The last work, the ***Nieuwenhove diptych***, is a rare example of a medieval diptych that remains undivided. Painted in 1487, the young donor and subject of one of the two panels, Martin van Nieuwenhove, was only 23 years old at the time. One wonders if he had been nursed back to health by the sisters of St Juliaanshospitaal and presented the work in appreciation.

There is a tradition that Memling had been wounded at the Battle of Nancy in 1477, fighting for Charles the Bold, whom he certainly knew, and that he was cared for at Sint Janshospitaal. If true, it would explain how the brothers and sisters had been able to afford to commission four works from such a famous, and presumably expensive, painter. All were completed within the 3 years that followed the Battle of Nancy, and, as has been said, Memling depicted a patient of the hospital, possibly himself, in the Adoration of the Magi triptych: perhaps, therefore, the story is true.

From the hospital, Mariastraat continues southward, merging with Katelijnestraat, an important, but not particularly interesting shopping street. Nieuwe Gentweg, second left, possesses one of the longest unbroken stretches of almshouses in Bruges, where two establishments: **Godshuis Sint Jozef** (1674) and **Godshuis Meulenaere** (1613) merge between 8 and 24. The beautifully maintained courtyard garden of the latter may be entered from the splendid Baroque portal. Much of the charm of Bruges is dependant on its ancient almshouses, originally built by philanthropic citizens to provide basic accommodation for the destitute. There are still fifty in existence, all now modernized internally and managed by the state.

Further along the street, at number 53, is **De Snippe**, a hotel/restaurant which, although unprepossessing externally, serves some of the finest cuisine in Bruges, concentrating on French specialities, particularly fish. Its restaurant is a delight, with delicate murals and splendid chandeliers of Murano glass.

A return westward leads to Drie Kroezenstraat, left, where, at its south end, the seven gables of **Godshuis Onze-Lieve Vrouwe der**

Following page: The Meulenaere almshouse, built in 1613, is typical of the fifty similar establishments which still survive in Bruges

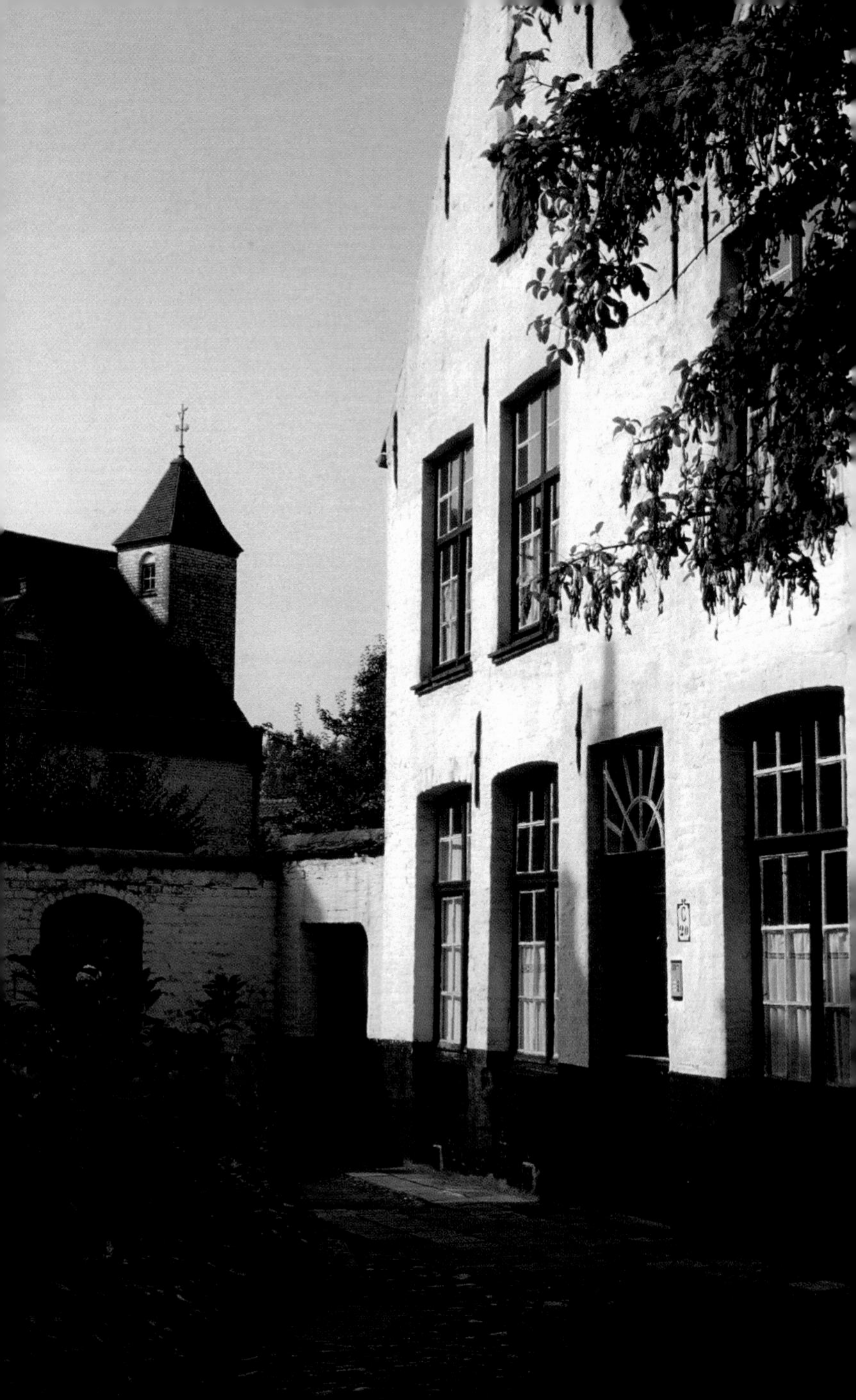

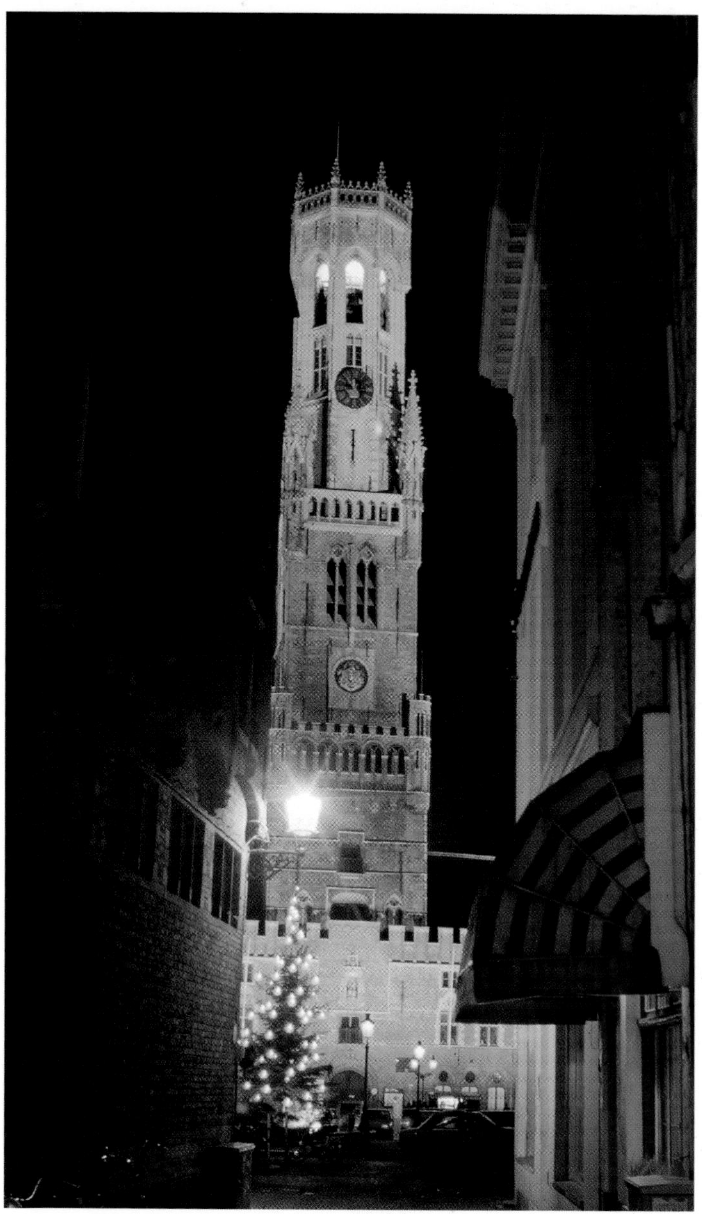

Zeven Ween (Almshouse of the Virgin of the Seven Sorrows) were the inspiration for its name. On the Baroque portal is inscribed the date 1654.

Oude Gentweg, right, brings us back to Katelijnestraat, right, from where Walstraat, first left, leads to the always lively **Walplein**, a rectangular-shaped square almost entirely devoted to tourist bars and restaurants. **De Zevende Hemel** (Seventh Heaven) restaurant occupies an ancient step-gabled house. Directly opposite, nestling beneath the trees, the bronze group is entitled *Leda, Pegasus, Prometheus and Zeus*, but there was no sign of Zeus at the time of writing — perhaps he was having a quick drink from one of the many beer mugs collected by *Jantje van Pardoens*, the next bar!

On the opposite side of the square is one of the few breweries still functioning in Bruges, **De Halve Maan** (Half Moon). This trademark derived from the name of the Bruges house that brewer Henri Maes first occupied in 1564. Incidentally, by tradition, the first son born to each generation of the Maes family is called Henri. Visits may be made to the brewery at the rear, which was founded here in 1856 to produce Straffe Hendrik, a speciality beer with a very pronounced flavour — as may be expected, tastings are included in the admission price. Vast quantities of Straffe Hendrik beer are available, not only in Bruges, but throughout much of Belgium; most of it, however, comes from a much larger brewery located elsewhere in West Flanders.

From the south end of the square, **Wijngaardstraat**, right, leads to the bridge that faces the Begijnhof. Although short, Wijngaardstraat has a wide selection of restaurants, some of them offering reasonably-priced table d'hôte menus, not easily found elsewhere in Bruges.

Before continuing ahead to the Begijnhof, a short detour southward along Noordstraat (virtually a continuation of Walplein) leads to an exceptionally picturesque group of almshouses, **Het Godshuis De Vos**, built around an open courtyard in 1713, and immaculately restored in 1995; its tiny, private chapel has survived.

Ahead, on the Arsenaalstraat corner of Noordstraat, rises an enormous **medieval chimney** with a vaulted cooking recess. The structure is a sixteenth-century remnant (with twentieth-century buttresses) of the former Bogarden Convent that once stood here. It now lies on the fringe of the nineteenth-century complex of buildings housing the **Academy of Fine Arts**, formerly located in the Poortersloge in what is still called Academiestraat.

On returning to Wijngaardstraat, take the right fork at its west end and cross the bridge to the pedimented Classical gateway of the **Begijnhof**, (or Beguinage, its French name)

Preceding page: Nightime illumination gives the Belfry a fairytale appearance

dated 1776 and restored in 1995. Within a niche stands a figure of St Elizabeth of Hungary, patron of the foundation.

After the belfry and the town hall, the Begijnhof is the best-known venerable location in Bruges. It resembles a large almshouse, with small dwellings and a church surrounding a tree-studded green.

As was to reoccur after World War I, unspeakable carnage during the wars of the Crusades meant that many young women in Europe were widowed, and unmarried maidens had little prospect of marriage unless they were exceptionally comely or hailed from a wealthy family. Great hardship was to ensue. In order to care for these destitute women, Lambert le Bègue, a Liège priest, founded the charitable Order of the Beguines around 1189. Nothing survives of the first beguinage, at Liège, but in the thirteenth century, two of Boudewijn of Constantinople's daughters, Margaret and Joanna, revived the concept by setting up beguinages at Ghent, Antwerp, Leuven, Kortrijk, Lier and Amsterdam. Margaret of Constantinople, Countess of Flanders, founded the Bruges Begijnhof around 1245, a century before a similar development, which also survives, was established at Amsterdam. Although not strictly monastic, the Begijnhof accommodated women who were willing to follow a convent lifestyle but without fully committing themselves to it. Some took vows of chastity, but were permitted to leave and marry if they changed their minds. They were not idle: at Bruges their tasks included lace making or caring for children and the sick, under the direction of the *grootjuffrouw* (Great Lady).

The Begijnhof is particularly attractive in early spring, when a myriad of daffodils bloom: Winston Churchill loved to paint the scene. At Ghent and Amsterdam, the houses of their begijnhofs are similarly grouped around a central green, but the other examples in Belgium are planned as a series of narrow, interconnecting streets.

Immediately after entering the complex, house number C1, to the left, may be visited. Once a begijn's dwelling, it now serves as a small museum (closed 12noon-3.45pm) in  which is displayed a painting of the annual sacrementa procession in the Begijnhof. No begijns have lived here since 1930, when the last died and they were replaced by the present occupants, sisters of the Benedictine Order, who still wear fifteenth-century habits.

The approach to the Begijnhof, it may be recalled, was made from Wijngardstraat (Vineyard Street), and the official name of the establishment is Prinselijk Begijnhof ten Wijngaarde (Princely Begijnhof of the Vineyard). 'Princely' refers to the adoption of the Order by the King of France, Philip the Fair, in 1299, but 'vineyard' puzzles many. The explanation is that the site was a *meer*, Dutch for marsh, which the French mistranslated as vineyard; one assumes that the marsh was drained soon after the begijns settled on it.

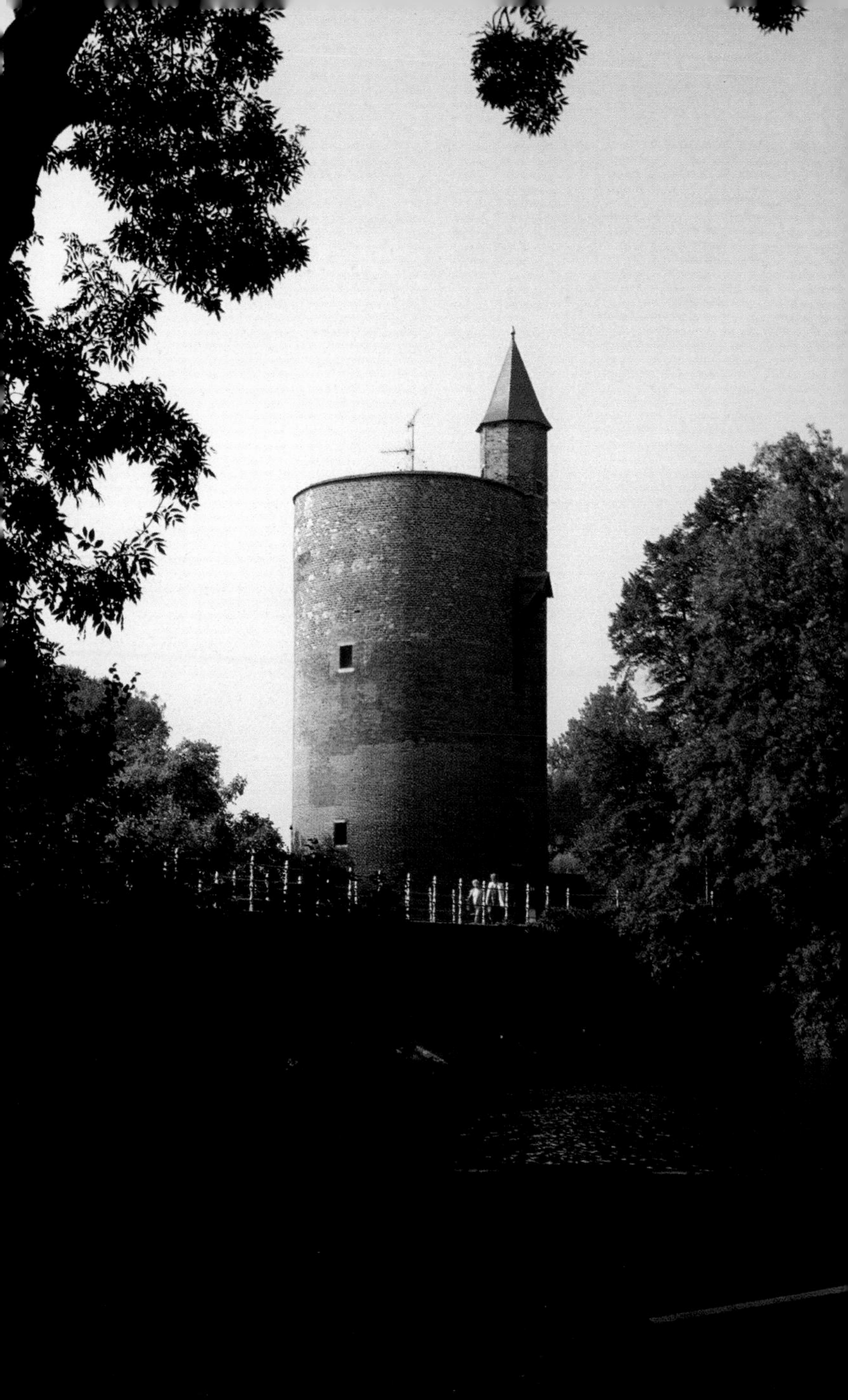

A pathway, from which each house and the church may be reached, encircles the green. The **Begijnhof church**, dedicated to St Elizabeth of Hungary, stands on the east side, its chancel facing the water. Founded in Burg as the chapel of the heir to the Count of Flanders, Margaret of Constantinople, Countess of Flanders, transferred its parish in 1245 to the newly-built Begijnhof. The earlier church was badly damaged by fire in 1584, and rebuilt in 1602.

St Elizabeth, depicted in a niche above the entrance, is also the subject of the most important work within the church, the altar painting by Jacob van Oost the Elder. An amusing and apparently truthful story refers to the book in the painting, which was added during restoration work in 1802 as replacement for a dog. The Grand Lady, it appears, decided that the animal, although small, was an undignified companion for the begijns' patron saint, and ordered the amendment.

The choir screen incorporates a piece of stone cut from the rock where the Virgin Mary is alleged to have made an appearance at Lourdes.

It will be noted that the houses, most of which date from the seventeenth and eighteenth centuries, vary in design, partly because all the originals have been replaced at different times. The Gothic style, however, has been maintained; C4, for example, exhibits pointed arches and foiled tracery, even though it was built in the seventeenth century. All, however, are whitewashed and retain wrought-iron bell pulls. One house, near the church, and considerably larger than the others, was the residence of the Grand Lady.

A return through the main gateway of the Begijnhof and a right turn after the bridge has been crossed leads to **Minnewater**, a lake created around 1200 to form a harbour for craft using the Lieve Canal to Ghent. Sluices near the present Sashuis (sluice house) probably formed the first barrier. Views, which are extremely romantic in any case, are enhanced by swans gliding sedately on the waters. However, it is certain that Minnewater does not mean 'Lake of Love', as is popularly supposed. A more likely translation is Inner Harbour, but it has been suggested that *minne* referred to a boat turning round to leave the harbour.

To explore Minnewater, follow the path on the west side towards the bridge.

Adjoining **Minnewaterpark**, located on the east side of the lake, can be seen a nineteenth-century mock-Gothic castle, now a top class restaurant. The park and restaurant can both be reached from Arsenaalstraat.

Twin towers were built by Jan van Oudenaarde for defensive purposes at the south end of the rectangular lake, which interrupted the city wall

Facing page: Poertoren (Powder Tower) was built in 1398 to protect the entry to Minnewater, which formed a breach in the city wall. Its name came from the gunpowder stored within the tower

at this point. One of the towers survives in its entirety, **Poertoren** (Powder Tower), built in 1398, and so-named because gunpowder and weapons were stored within it. Most of the other tower, constructed 3 years later, was demolished around 1621; however, its base, which still exists, served as an ice house from 1780 to 1914.

The bridge was constructed in 1740, originally with an unobstructed central span to permit the passage of high vessels, in particular a barge, which was towed by horses regularly between Bruges and Ghent. The central arch is, therefore, a later addition.

Some weary visitors may now be relieved to hear that this lengthy excursion is now almost at an end, the **railway/bus station** only being a few minutes walk away. This is reached by turning right at the Poertoren and following Begijnvest westward. At its end turn left and continue ahead to Stationsplein.

Additional Information

Places to Visit

Begijnhof Museum
Begijnhof (Bèguinage)
Open: December, January and February. Wednesday, Thursday, Saturday and Sunday 2.45-4.15pm. Friday 1.45-6pm. March, October to November: 10.30am-12noon, 1.45-5pm. April-September: 10am-12noon, 1.45-7.30pm (Sunday 6pm).

Belfry
7 Markt
Open: 1 April-30 September 9.30am-5pm. 1 October-31 March 9.30am-12.30pm, 1.30-5pm.

Groeninge Museum
12 Dijver
Open: 1 April-30 September 9.30am-5pm. 1 October-31 March 9.30am-12.30pm, 2-5pm. Closed Tuesday.

Gruuthuse Museum
17 Dijver
Open: 1 April-30 September 9.30am-5pm. 1 October-31 March 9.30am-12.30pm, 2-5pm. Closed Tuesday.

Heilig Bloed Basiliek (Holy Blood Basilica)
13 Burg
Open: 1 April-30 September 9.30am-12noon, 2-6pm. 1 October-31 March 10am-12noon, 2-4pm.

Kantmuseum (Lace Museum) and Brangwyn Museum
16 Dijver
Open: 1 April-30 September 9.30am-5pm. 1 October-31 March 9.30am-12.30pm, 2-5pm. Closed Tuesday.

Lace Centre
3A Peperstraat
Open: 1 April-30 September 10am-12noon, 2-6pm. 1 October-31 March 10am-12noon, 2-5pm. Closed on Sunday. Demonstrations every afternoon.

Onze-Lieve-Vrouwekerk (Church of Our Lady)
O.L.V Kerkhof Zuid
Open: 1 April-30 September 10-11.30am, 2.30-5pm, Sunday 2.30-5pm, Saturday 10-11.30am, 2.30-4pm. 1 October-31 March 10.00-11.30am, 2-4pm, Sunday 2.30-4.30pm, Saturday 10-11.30am, 2.30-4pm.

Provinciaal Museum Het Brugse Vrije
11A Burg
Open: 1 April-30 September 10am-12noon, 1-5pm. Closed Monday. 1 October-31 March (not January) 10am-12noon, 1.30-5pm. Closed Monday.

Sint Janshospitaal (St John's Hospital) and Memling Museum
38 Mariastraat
Open: 1 April-30 September 9.30am-5pm. 1 October-31 March 9.30am-12.30pm, 2-5pm. Closed Wednesday.

Straffe Hendrik (Brewery Tour)
26 Walplein
Open: 1 April-30 September 10am-5pm (continuously). Groups on request (☎ 050 33 26 97)
1 October-31 March 11am and 3pm.

Straffe Hendrik (Brewery Museum)
26 Walplein
Open: 1 June-30 September, Wednesday-Sunday 2-5pm.

North-East Bru

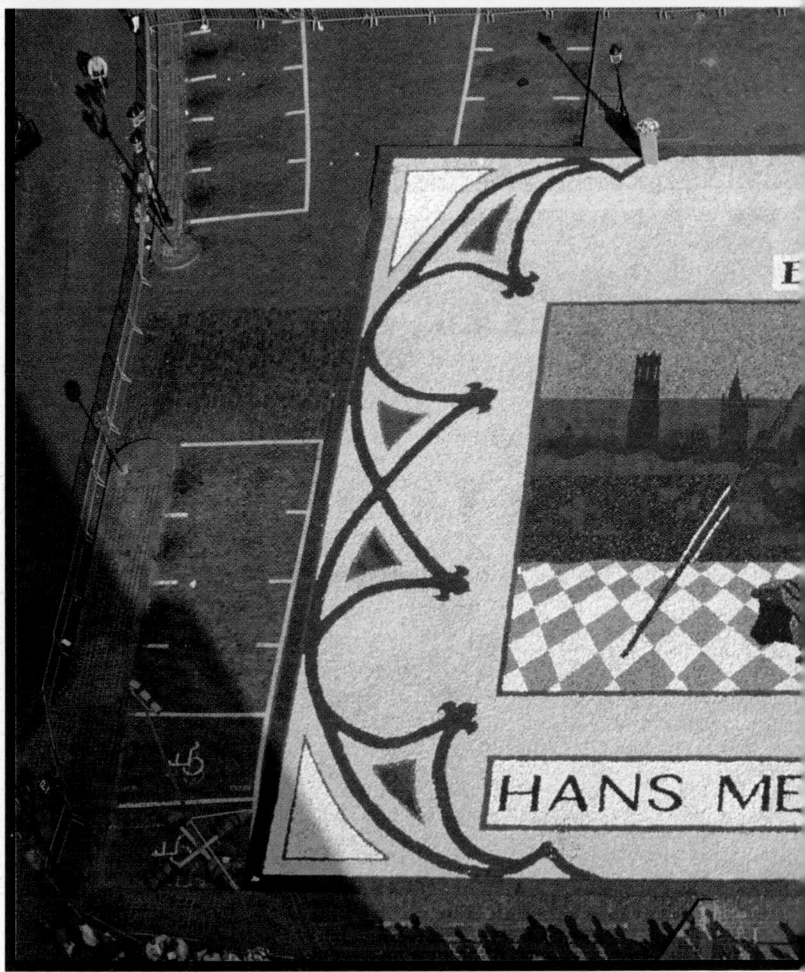

s

2

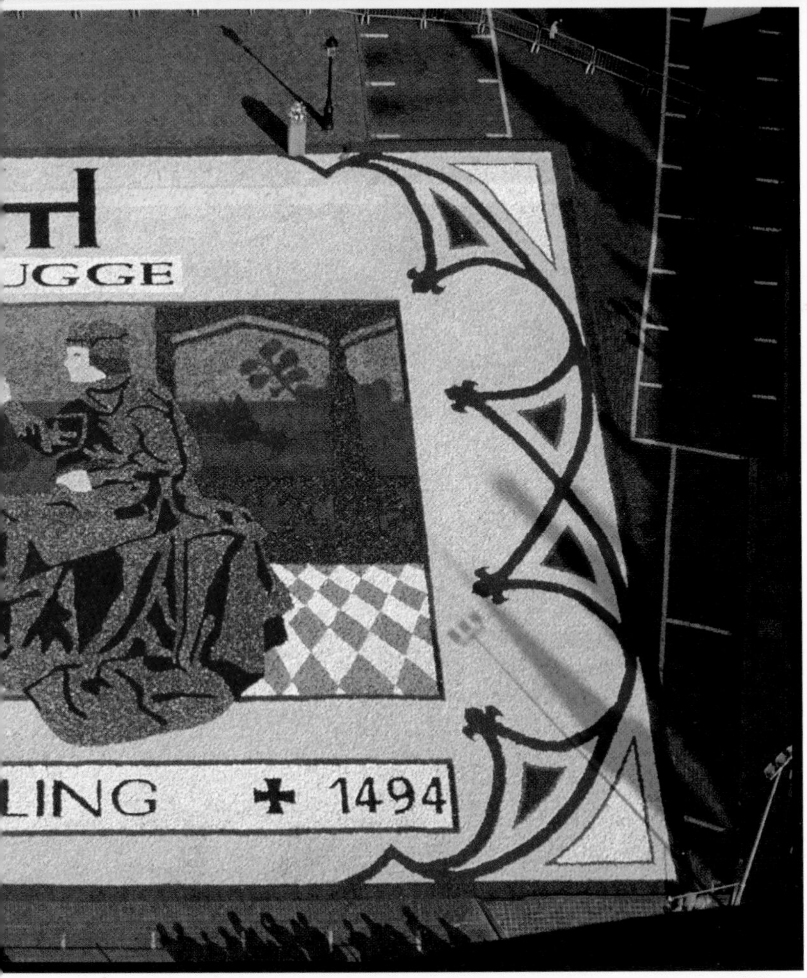

Churches, Museums and Windmills

Starting and ending at Markt, this itinerary includes some of the finest churches in Bruges, all with Gothic exteriors and mainly Baroque interiors. Not to be missed are the O-L-V Potterie hospital and the premises of the St Sebastian's Guild, in which are displayed several exhibits emphasising the guild's close ties with British monarchs. The route followed, which will be much less crowded with tourists, may be completed in half a day — as long as not too much time is spent in the brewery and taverns passed on route!

From the north end of **Markt** follow Philipstockstraat eastward. On the left is the church known as **Het Keerske**. Founded in 1080 as the double chapel of the Chandlers Guild (hence its name, which means the Candle), dedicated to St Peter and St Katherine, it was entirely rebuilt in 1725 and heavily restored in 1987. Whilst the interior is of no greater architectural interest than the exterior, some English visitors may wish to enter, as it is here that Church of England services in Bruges are held every Sunday at 6pm.

When Burg is reached, cross between the trees to the south side and the bridged **Blinde Ezelstraat**. The strange name of this street, meaning Blind Donkey, is a reference to an eponymous tavern owned by the bishop, which once stood in the narrow thoroughfare. Apparently, the cheapest beer in the city was served within, and many patrons became 'blind donkeys', an expression for drunkards. A rather nastier story about the derivation of the street's name, almost certainly untrue, is told of a trader's donkey that repeatedly refused to go down the street because something he saw there frightened him; to overcome this, the owner blinded the poor creature.

Before proceeding beneath the arch, note, immediately right, on the façade of **Stadhuis**, a carved figure of the Virgin of Ourdenaarde. She holds an inkwell, as did both earlier statues of her, and was adopted as their patron by the Clerical Guild. In order to protect the rather exposed figure, a cage was fixed around it, as can be seen from contemporary paintings of Burg. This expediency, however, failed to save the carving from French revolutionary iconoclasts, and, like the other examples, this piece of sculpture is recent work.

At the end of Blinde Ezelstraat, a right turn leads to one of the most photogenic squares in Bruges, **Huidenvettersplein**. Artists may be seen, some of them occasionally working on their 'masterpieces', and the ambience resembles a miniature version of Place du Tertre in the Montmartre quarter of Paris.

The buildings of greatest interest line the west side, all of them backing

Preceding pages: Flower 'tapestries' are laid in Markt on special occasions; this example commemorated the Memling Exhibition of 1994

the canal, and all of them possessing restaurants. **Hotel Duc de Bourgogne**, built in 1648, has two stepped gables. **Huidenvettershuis**, dated 1630, is castellated and now forms part of 't Dreveken restaurant, the first section of which dates from the rebuilding of 1664. This was originally the guildhouse of the *huidenvetters* (tanners), and aspects of their trade are depicted in the bas-reliefs of the façade. Restaurant specialities include rabbit with prunes, and chicken casserolled in beer.

From the south side of the square, more steps descending to the waterside indicate another staging point for boat trips. Ahead, the view across the water to the belfry from Rozenhoedkaai is the most famous in Bruges.

Rozenhoedkaai (Rosary Quay) refers to the rosaries' beads of ivory and amber that were once sold here to devout Catholics. Rainer Maria Rilke (1874-1965) dedicated his work *Quai de Rosaire* to the quay. In earlier times, the thoroughfare was called Zoutkaai (Salt Quay), as great quantities of salt from France and Germany were unloaded there.

From Rozenhoedkaai it may be observed that the rear of Huidenvettershuis, is step-gabled, rather than castellated like its front. At the Nepomucenus Bridge end of the quay, above seven windows of the first house on the south side, lunettes are carved with bas-reliefs depicting the Seven Acts of Mercy.

Return towards Pandreitje, which continues southward from Huidenvettersplein, passing the west side of a small park, the splendid trees of which frame views of the belfry. Perhaps only a few will wish to continue southward to observe the monumental nineteenth-century gateway, all that survives of the state prison. The remainder of the large, now empty, site awaits redevelopment, possibly to accommodate a luxury hotel.

The name Pand (in Pandreitje), meaning Pawn, derives from the stand of the jewellers and goldsmiths that was erected annually on part of the future site of the prison for the Bruges spring fair until, in 1671, a house of correction, primarily for vagabonds, was built. On conversion to a state prison in 1827, the adjacent **Vleeshuis** (Meathouse) of the master butchers was incorporated, and most of the complex rebuilt; the gatehouse dates from this period.

If Pandreitje is followed, it will lead to Gevangenisstraat, followed by the street simply called Park, as it overlooks **Koningin Astrid Park**, the former grounds of a Franciscan monastery, now the most popular open space in the city centre. Its name commemorates the much-loved Swedish-born Queen Astrid, consort of King Leopold III. During a visit to Switzerland in 1935, the King was driving his car, which crashed, killing Astrid. Heavy mourning throughout Belgium followed, many blaming the unfortunate Leopold for the tragedy. The Queen's statue may be seen at the north-west end of the enclosure.

One of the most attractive bars in

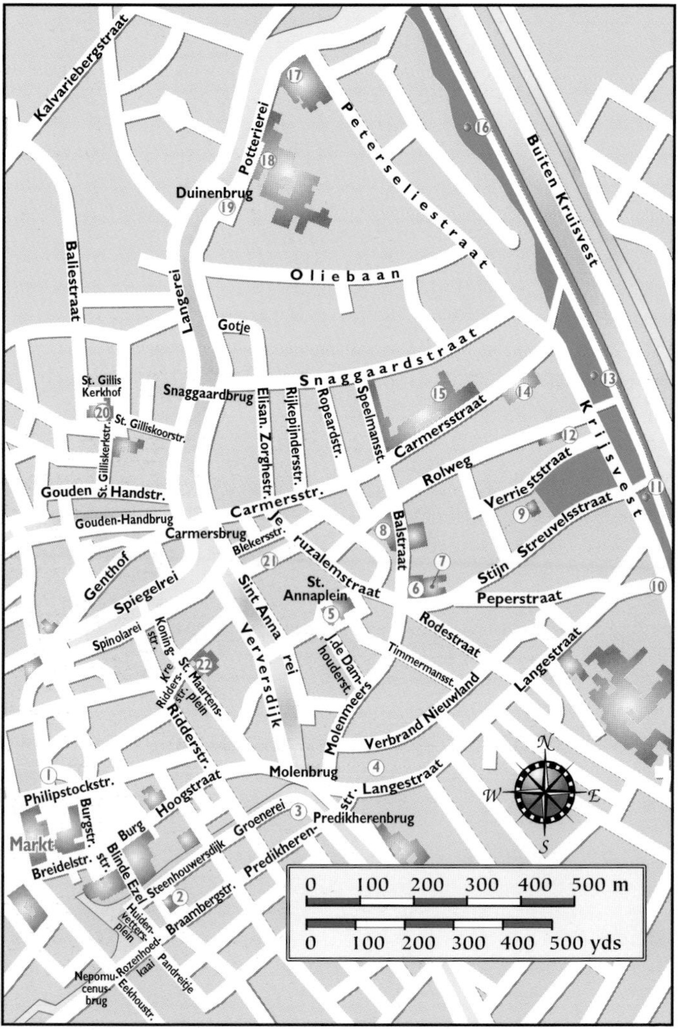

Bruges stands on the north side of the park, **L'Estaminet**. Beamed ceilings and hops give a venerable appearance to the interior, rare in Bruges. Outside, there is an open terrace, ingeniously designed so that the canopy and glass partitions can be entirely removed in winter. The bar is shut all day Thursday, and Monday after 2pm.

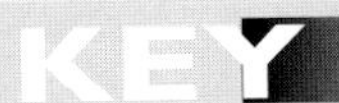

1. Het Keerske (Anglican Church)
2. Fish Market (Vismarkt)
3. Godshuis de Pelikaan (almshouses)
4. De Gouden Boom (Brewery and Malthouse Museum)
5. St Anne's Church (Sint Annakerk)
6. Jerusalem Church (Jeruzalemkerk)
7. Lace Centre (Kantcentrum)
8. Folklore Museum (Museum voor Volkskunde)
9. St George's Guild (Sint Jorisgilde)
10. Kruispoort (city gate)
11. Bonne Chiere (windmill-not working)
12. Guido Gezellemuseum
13. Sint Janshuysmolen (windmill-working in summer)
14. St Sebastian's Guild (Sint Sebastiaansgilde)
15. English Convent (Engels Klooster)
16. De Nieuwe Papegaai (windmill-not working)
17. Our Lady of the Pottery (museum) Onze-Lieve-Vrouw ter Potterie
18. Episcopal Seminary
19. Duinenbrug (wooden bridge)
20. St Giles Church (Sint Gilliskerk)
21. Vlissinghe (ancient tavern)
22. St Walburga Church (Sint Walburgakerk)

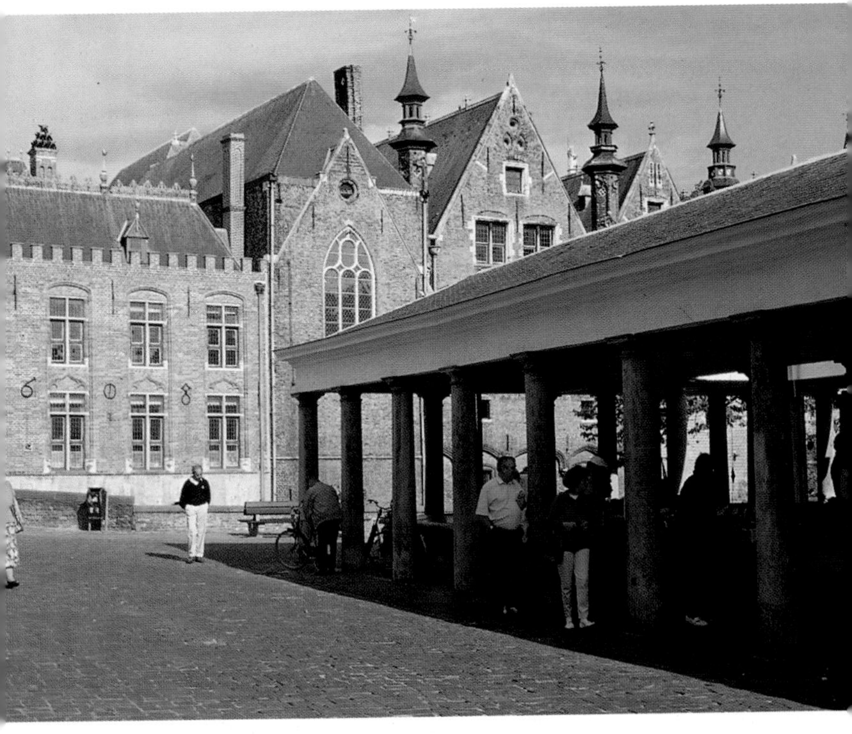

Vismarkt is at its liveliest Wednesdays and Fridays; bars and fish restaurants surround it

From the north-west corner of the park, Jozef Suveestraat leads northward to Vismarkt. Those who have not visited Koningin Astrid Park may reach Vismarkt by returning eastward along Rozenhoedkaai to Braambergstraat, which skirts its south side.

Vismarkt (Fish Market) occupies stalls grouped permanently around a central courtyard, in which stands an enormous water pump. Tuscan colonnades support roofs that give some protection from the weather. The complex was built, in Classical style, by the municipal architect in 1826, and is the only public development of importance in Bruges dating from the brief period when Belgium and Holland were reunited (1815-30). The Bruges fish market had occupied part of the north side of Markt until 1745. Wednesday and Friday mornings are the liveliest times to visit; little is left by midday, and the market closes Sunday and Monday. As may be expected, there are several bars and fish restaurants grouped around the Vismarkt.

Braambergstraat continues eastward from the south end of the square. At number 7, the former trading house of the Fishporters, built in 1637, has been converted to a tavern called **De Kogge** (The Fishbasket). On the façade, two stones are carved to depict fish porters. A simple, woody interior, with an old fireplace and a gallery, has given De Kooge the most ancient and unspoiled appearance of all the taverns in Bruges.

A return to the east side of Vismarkt will conduct us northward to Steenhouwersdijk, from where there are splendid views across the canal to the fifteenth-century Gothic gables of the **Brugse Vrije**, which were spared when the range facing Burg was rebuilt in the eighteenth century. It is pleasant to follow the canal eastward to where the street that follows it becomes Groenerei and curves sharply southward.

Best viewed from Peerdenbrug, the bridge ahead, are the five linked almshouses at 8-12 Groenerei, each with its dormer window, that comprise **Godshuis de Pelikaan**, founded in 1634. Look for the relief above a doorway of a pelican feeding its young with its own blood (a Christian symbol of charity).

At Predikherenbrug, the canal leading southward is known as **Coupure**. It was excavated in the mid-eighteenth century, and flows towards the river in a straight line for ease of navigation. The stretch now provides moorings for pleasure craft.

From the opposite side of the bridge, Molenmeers curves northward. In Verbrand Nieuwland, first right, visitors may enter the gate at number 10 for guided tours of **De Gouden Boom (Golden Tree) Brewery** and/or visits to its museum.

The brewery was established in 1587, but its present buildings date from the early years of the twentieth century. Brewed here are Abdij Steenbrugge, Brugs Tarbier, a wheat beer sometimes drunk with a slice of lemon, and the very strong Brugse Tripel (9.5%) with a rather sweet flavour.

The museum is located in the former Malthouse; exhibits include brewing machinery, barrels, bottles, ancient documents and a reconstructed Bruges café of around 1900. Visitors to the brewery itself are shown the entire brewing process from grain delivery to the final product. All are given a glass of beer.

From the brewery, return to Molenmeers, turn right and take the second turning left, Joost de Damhouderstraat, to Sint Annaplein.

Within the square stands **Sint Annakerk** (St Anne's Church), a 1624 rebuilding of an earlier church founded in 1497 but completely destroyed in 1586 during the period of religious strife.

Externally, the brick building is basically an undemonstrative example of the late-Gothic style; however, it can be seen that the windows of the nave were originally larger.

On entering Sint Annakerk (May-September only) it is immediately revealed that the interior is Baroque, rather than the expected Gothic. With its dark oak, chancel screen and brass chandeliers, the appearance is reminiscent of one of Sir Christopher Wren's more ambitious City of London churches. Flemish carving had reached its high point when the church was built, and there are masterly examples throughout. Unusually exuberant is the woodwork of the nave, with its range of barleysugar pilasters. The pulpit, confessionals and stalls are all crisply carved, but it is perhaps the marble rood screen between the nave and the chancel that most takes the eye, with its gleaming brass mounts.

Above the exit, at the west end, the *Last Judgement* mural was painted by Herregoudts in 1685.

From the rear of Sint Annakerk, Jeruzalemstraat, right, stretches eastward to Peperstraat, on the corner of which stands the most eccentric church in Bruges, little-altered since it was built.

Jeruzalemkerk (Jerusalem Church) was founded around 1427 by Pieter and Jacob Adornes, descendants of a thirteenth-century Genoese merchant who had settled in Bruges after taking part in the crusades. It was built for the private use of the Adornes family. Anselm Adornes, the son of Pieter, returned from Jerusalem with relics, many of which survive in the building.

Entered from the south side, the church consists of three separate chapels, two of them on the ground floor, the third occupying the high-ceilinged upper storey. By tradition, Jeruzalemkerk was modelled on the Church of the Holy Sepulchre in Jerusalem, which the crusading Anselms would have seen, and this is the reason for its name. Most are surprised by the compactness of the building, which only becomes apparent after it has been entered.

The unusually low, black marble tombchest of Anselm Adornes and his wife Margarethe, surmounted by

Following page: Blinde Ezelstraat seen from the canal. The picturesque roofline in the background is the rear of the Stadhuis

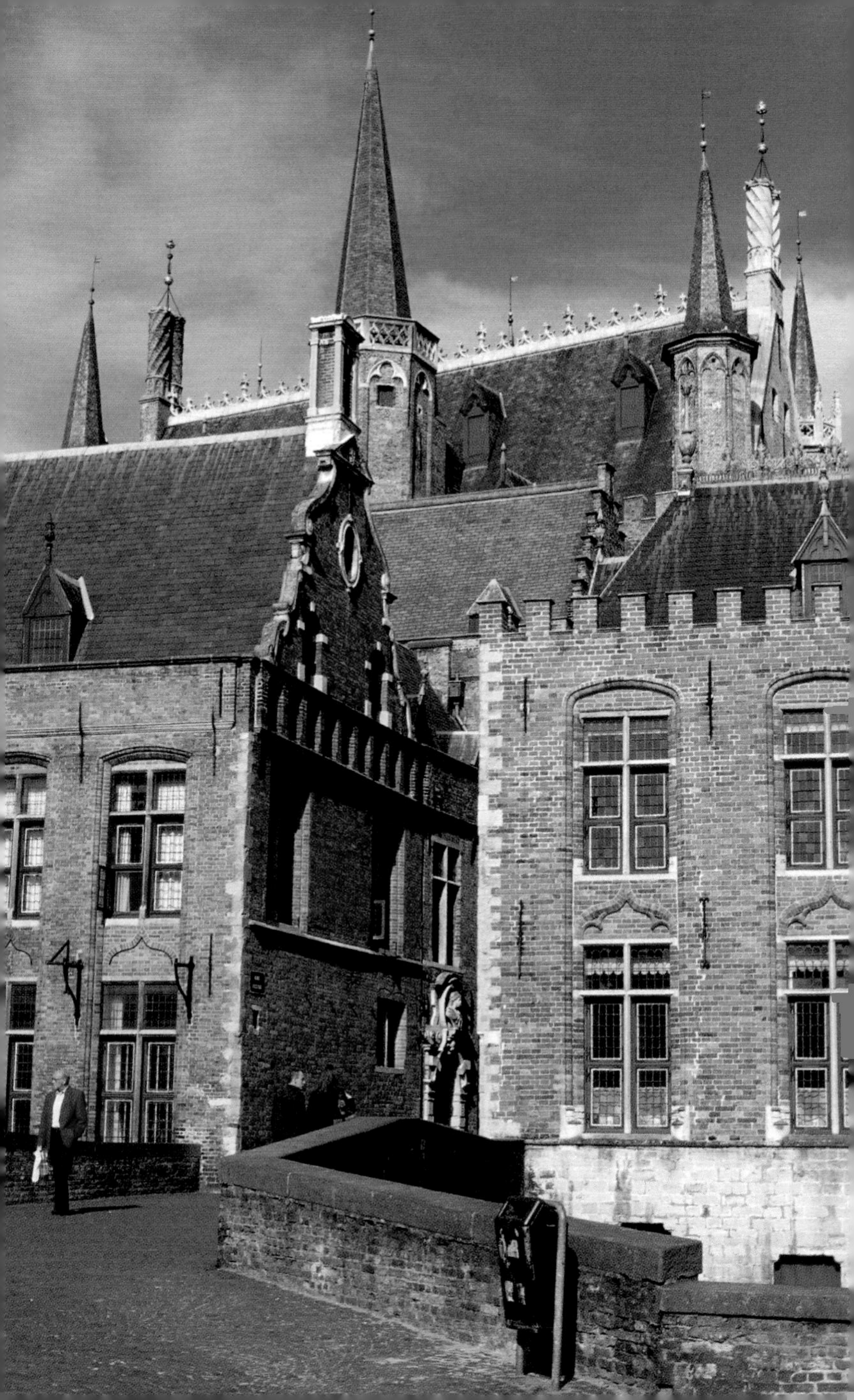

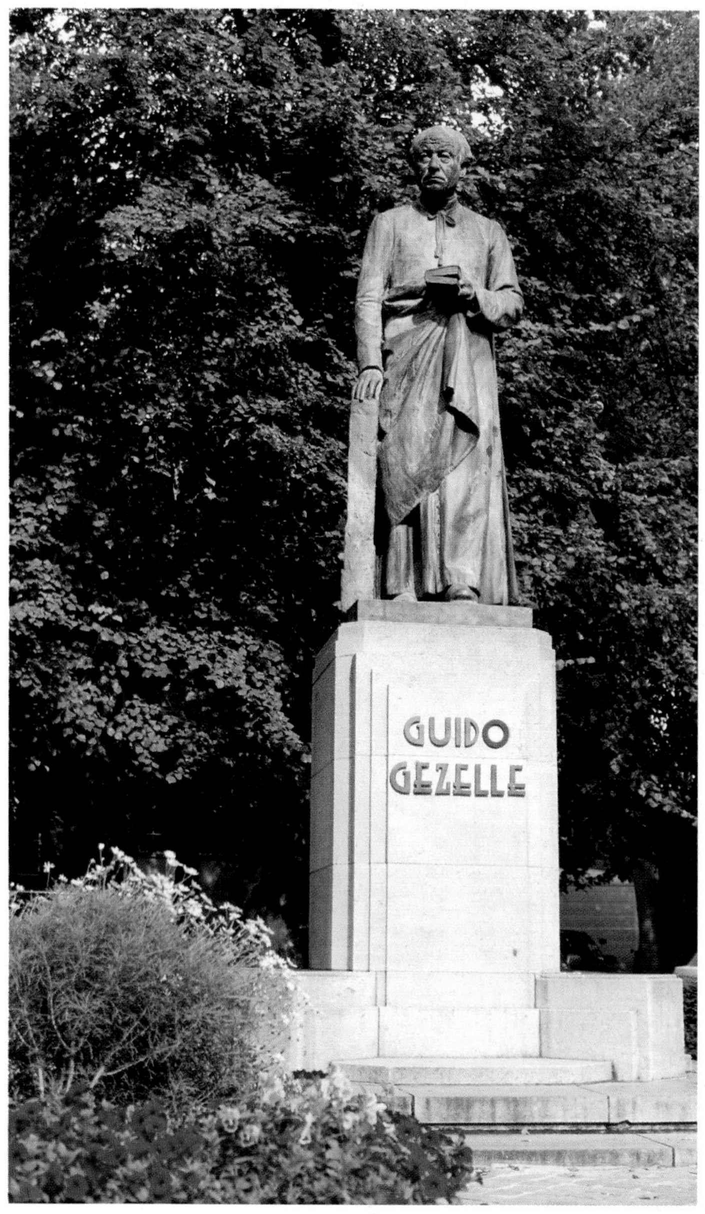
GUIDO
GEZELLE

their recumbent figures, stands in the entrance chapel; Gothic lettering on the sides is now hard to decipher. Anselm Adornes, who served as a diplomat for the Duke of Burgundy, was asked by King James III of Scotland to look after the interests of Scottish wool traders in Flanders. During a visit to Scotland, Adornes was murdered, 23 January 1483, and buried in Linlithgow Palace. All that lies in Anselm's tombchest is his heart, which was brought to Bruges.

Stained glass windows, dated 1432, and wall monuments commemorate members of the family, which still owns the church. The Adornes emblem of a wheel and a halo will be noted.

In the small side chapel is displayed a model of Jerusalem's Holy Sepulchre, incorporating a figure of Christ, and a gilded reliquary, said to contain a fragment of the Holy Cross.

The upper chapel, reached by the steps, may be viewed but not usually entered; its ceiling is surprisingly high for the area.

Next to the church, in Peperstraat, the Adornes family founded an almshouse, which has been converted to the **Kantcentrum** (Lace Centre). Every afternoon, except Sunday, approximately twenty women of various ages can be observed making bobbin lace; the intricate but confident movement of their hands can be quite hypnotic. Articles are sold, and unidentifed examples of lacework displayed.

Return to Jeruzalemkerk and follow Balstraat northward, passing, right, the Junior Lace School, at 16. On the Rolweg corner, at 40, is **Museum voor Volkskunde** (Folklore Museum).

The museum occupies a group of rooms in what was formerly the Shoemakers almshouse. Each is fitted out to represent an ancient Bruges shop or living area. Of particular interest are: **room 3** with its splendid display of copper moulds for use in the kitchen, the apothecary in **room 4**, and the collection of pipes in **room 14**.

Four locations of only marginal interest lie to the east, but those with sufficient time at their disposal may wish to see them. A return to Peperstraat, passing the Kantcentrum and following the street to its end, brings the visitor to **Kruispoort**, one of the ancient gateways of Bruges.

First erected in 1402, at the same time as Gentpoort, another gate that also survives to the south, Kruispoort was built of white sandstone rather than the usual brick; much rebuilding has taken place, and the gate was restored in 1972. All the gates of Bruges punctuated the defensive wall that was constructed on the city side of the river in the thirteenth and fourteenth centuries.

Kruisvest follows the riverbank northward, passing, right, the **Bonne Chiere Windmill**. Originally constructed in East Flanders in 1888, this windmill was re-erected on the Bruges

Preceding page: The statue of Guido Gezelle commemorates the great Flemish poet, whose birthplace is now a museum rampart in 1911 for picturesque reasons only and it was not restored to working order.

The windmill faces Stijn Streuvelsstraat, which leads south-westward from Kruisvest. Accommodated since 1958 in a modern building, at 59 Stijn Streuvelsstraat, is the **Sint Jorisgilde** (Guild of St George). Founded in 1321, this was one of the medieval guilds of crossbow archers that protected the city. King Charles II of England made a donation to the guild during his exile in Bruges following the Civil War.

If a member is present, it may be possible to see the guild's *Golden Book*, containing the signatures of the kings of Belgium and visiting heads of state.

In the **Shooting Room** is a magnificent collection of ancient crossbows. The guild's most important painting hangs behind the top table in the **Council Hall**: this depicts Albert Casimir of Austria, Prince of Poland, and Maria Christina, Princess of Hungary and Bohemia.

The original guildhouse, now a school, survives some distance away at 5 Hugo Losschaertstraat, off Sint Jorisstraat, which is a continuation northward of Vlamingstraat.

Of only very limited interest to non Dutch-speaking visitors is the **Guido Gezellemuseum** (Gezelle Museum). This is reached by returning to Kruisvest, left, and following Rolweg, second left, a short distance to number 4.

Guido Gezelle, Belgium's most famous lyric poet, was born in this house in 1830, coincidentally the year in which his country gained its independence. By 1854, he was teaching at a school in Roeselare, West Flanders, and ordained a priest the same year. Almost immediately, Gezelle began to write poetry, much of it a paeon to the beauty of nature, which, apart from the love of God, was to be his greatest inspiration.

It appears that the young priest found the attractions of his nubile pupils difficult to resist, and he was quietly transferred from Roeselare to Bruges in 1860 to become vice-principal and professor of philosophy to a recently founded Anglo/Belgian seminary. Gezelle was very much an anglophile, speaking English perfectly. He served as assistant priest at Sint Walburgakerk (1865-1872), and founded a literary magazine. Unable to keep his non-liberal views in check, Gezelle met with strong opposition and, dispirited, his health began to fail and he moved to Kortrijk, to become a chaplain. Fortunately, Gezelle's translation of Longfellow's epic poem *The Song of Hiawatha* into Dutch revived both his popularity and his health.

In the spring of 1899, Guido Gezelle returned once more to Bruges, having been appointed chaplain of the Engels Klooster (English Convent). During a brief visit to England the same year, Gezelle caught an infection and died shortly after his return to Bruges, 27 November 1899.

Following page: Located in Carmersstraat, this *Virgin and Child* figure is regarded as one of the finest in the city

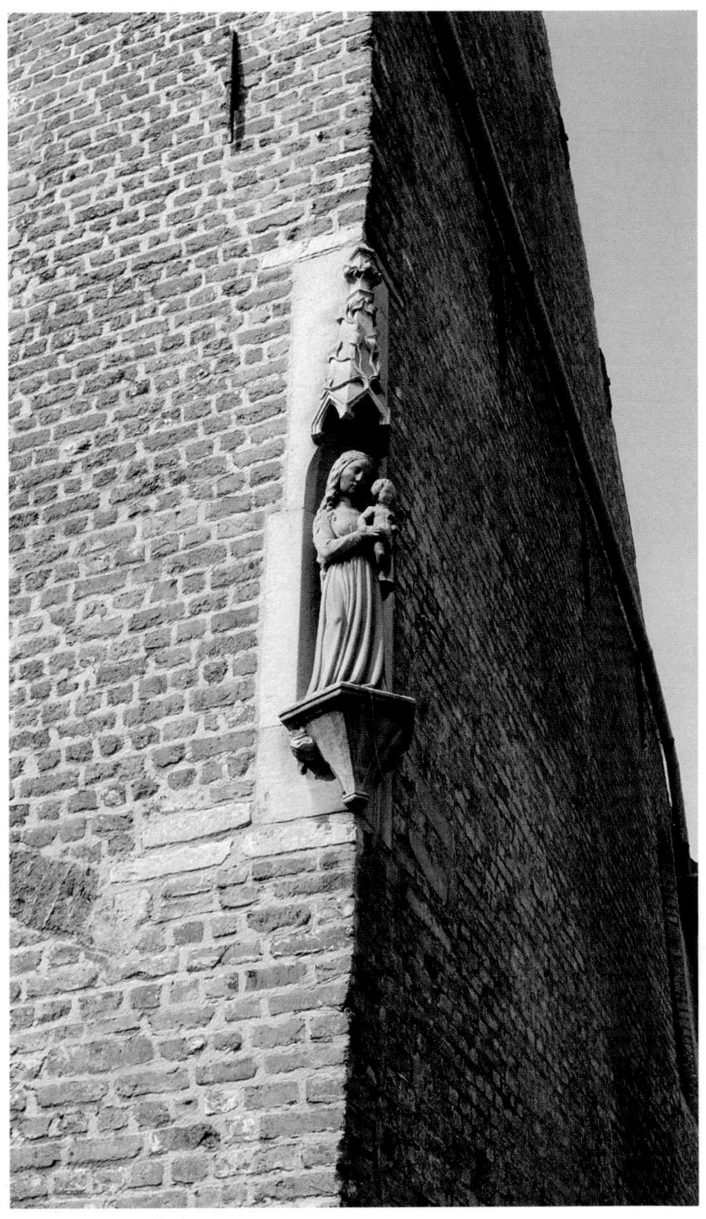

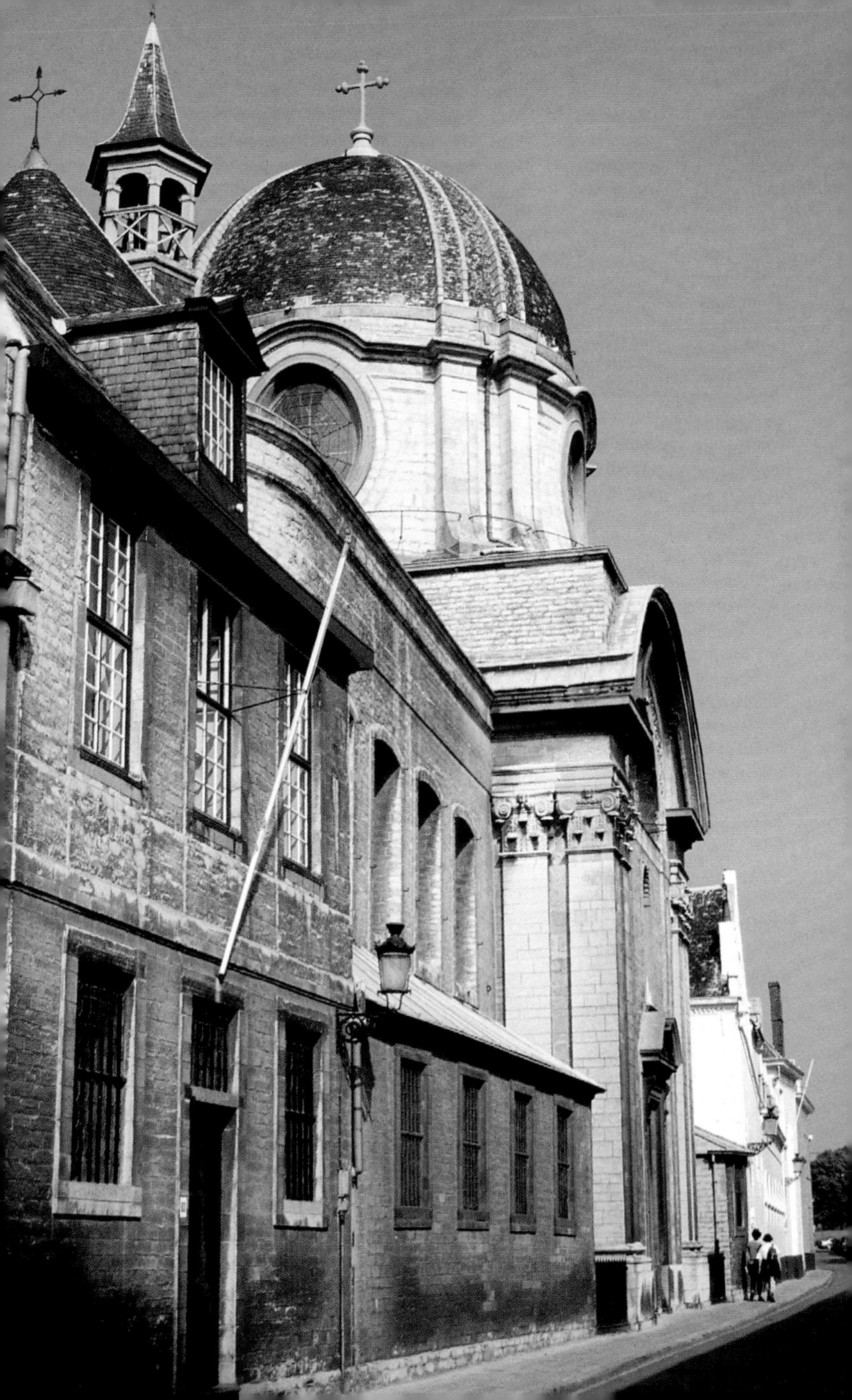

In 1926, three rooms in Gezelle's birthplace were converted to a museum, where memorabilia and various editions of the poet's work may be seen; some poems have been translated into English. On display is the pipe that Gezelle was extremely fond of smoking; by tradition, it broke the day before he died. There is a bust of Gezelle in the pleasant garden, which may be visited.

A perambulation westward along **Rolweg** leads back to the Museum voor Volkskunde, from where those who have not taken the diversion, as well as those who have, may proceed northward, following Korte Speelmansstraat to Carmersstraat, first right. At the junction, fitted in a niche in the building on the northwest corner, is a wooden *Virgin and Child* statue, carved in the eighteenth century, and one of the finest of around 500 religious figures that are still to be seen in the streets of Bruges.

Turn right along Carmersstraat, the name of which records the thirteenth-century Carmelite Convent that stood there for five centuries on the site of the present St Leo College (Potterierei). It was pulled down in 1584, rebuilt in the seventeenth century, and finally demolished in 1796.

A short distance further along Carmersstraat is the **Engels Klooster** (English Convent), at number 185. Rising from the complex can be seen the convent's domed church.

Since the reign of Queen Elizabeth I, life had been difficult for Catholics in England, and those who wished to lead a monastic life had to leave the country; many fled to the continent. The Convent of St Ursula at Leuven accepted novice nuns from England, who eventually founded their own Augustinian convent. In 1629, several hundred of them duly transferred to Bruges, occupying a large building called Nazareth. Catherine of Braganza, Portuguese-born consort of England's Charles II, and still a Catholic, presented the English Convent with her rosary and some valuable specimens of lace.

The first chapel was built here in 1650, but 6 years prior to this, Henry More, the great-grandson of Sir Thomas More, who had been executed by Henry VIII, was appointed visiting priest. Remaining in the possession of the Engels Klooster is a relic of Sir Thomas More, which Henry More presented to them. After Sir Thomas More's execution, his body is believed to have been interred in the Tower of London, but his head was kept by Margaret Roper, his daughter, at her house in Eltham; after her death, this was buried at St Dunstan, Canterbury. However, it appears that one of More's vertebrae was retained by his family as a relic, and it was this that Henry More donated to the sisters.

The present church was built in 1739 by the most Baroque of Bruges architects, Hendrik Pulinx; it is a rare Bruges example of a domed building.

Preceding page: The dome of the English Convent's church denotes Baroque work, only occasionally seen elsewhere in Bruges

As will be appreciated, the nuns had to flee Bruges at the French Revolution, most of them making their way to England, a country that had become much more tolerant of religious beliefs. Most returned in 1802, however, when Napoleon established religious freedom throughout his empire. Their convent, still known as Nazareth, had been sold in 1797, but the nuns were able to negotiate its return. English girls from wealthy Catholic families soon arrived to attend boarding school at the convent, and in 1887 a sister establishment was founded at Hampstead Heath, north London (this did not become autonomous until 1924). Guido Gezelle, rector for just 7 months, died at the Engels Klooster in 1899. It is said that his last words were 'I loved so much to hear the birds sing'.

Visitors are conducted to the chancel via a cloister, which was rebuilt in 1960 as a reproduction of the 1640 original. Apparently, the cupola was specified for acoustic reasons; its painting depicts the Apotheosis of St Augustine.

Those who did not visit the Sint Jorisgilde, and those who did but were disappointed, should not neglect to continue eastward to the Sint Sebastiaansgilde, at 147 Carmersstraat, accommodated in one of the most picturesque Gothic buildings in Bruges. Another medieval archers foundation — this time longbow archers, the **Sint**

Sebastiaansgilde (Guild of St Sebastian), founded in the fourteenth century, has occupied these premises since 1573. The guild played an important part in the Crusades, and for that reason the Cross of Jerusalem is incorporated in its arms.

The building has been referred to as the 'Cradle of the Grenadier Guards', as it was here that England's Charles II founded that regiment in 1656 while still exiled in Bruges. The King himself participated in archery contests, which took place in the grounds in fine weather or within the long gallery during the winter months. Guild members, restricted to 100, now meet primarily for social events, but many still practise their archery and participate in contests; every British sovereign since Charles II has been a member.

A beautifully proportioned polygonal tower, with an attached circular stairwell, rises beside the main, step-gabled building. Personal audio commentaries, available in several languages, fully describe the history of the guild and its possessions. The **Banqueting Hall** is of greatest interest, pride of place amongst the treasures displayed being given to the marble bust of Charles II, sculpted by Francois-Christophe Dieussart in 1666. Queen Victoria and Prince Albert presented the guild with a silver cup on their visit here in 1863, which is always on display. In more recent times, Queen Elizabeth II and the Duke of Edinburgh maintained the tradition of United Kingdon sovereigns present-

Following page: The octagonal Gothic tower of the Sint Sebastiaansgilde is a landmark in east Bruges

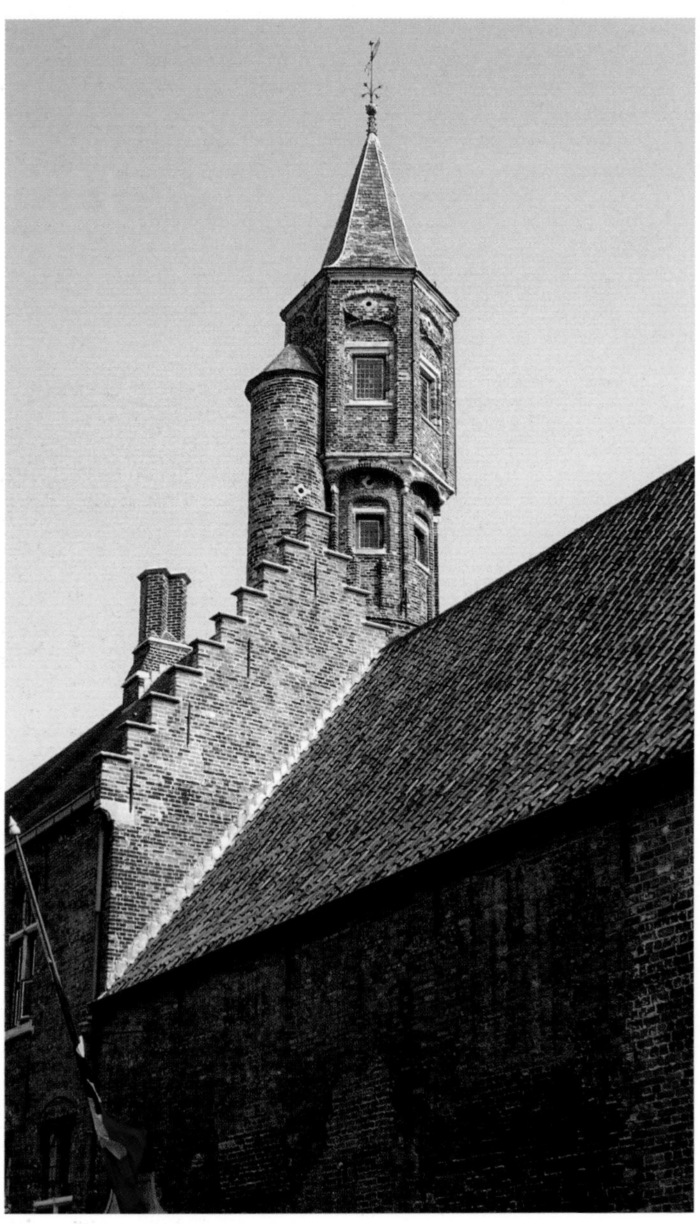

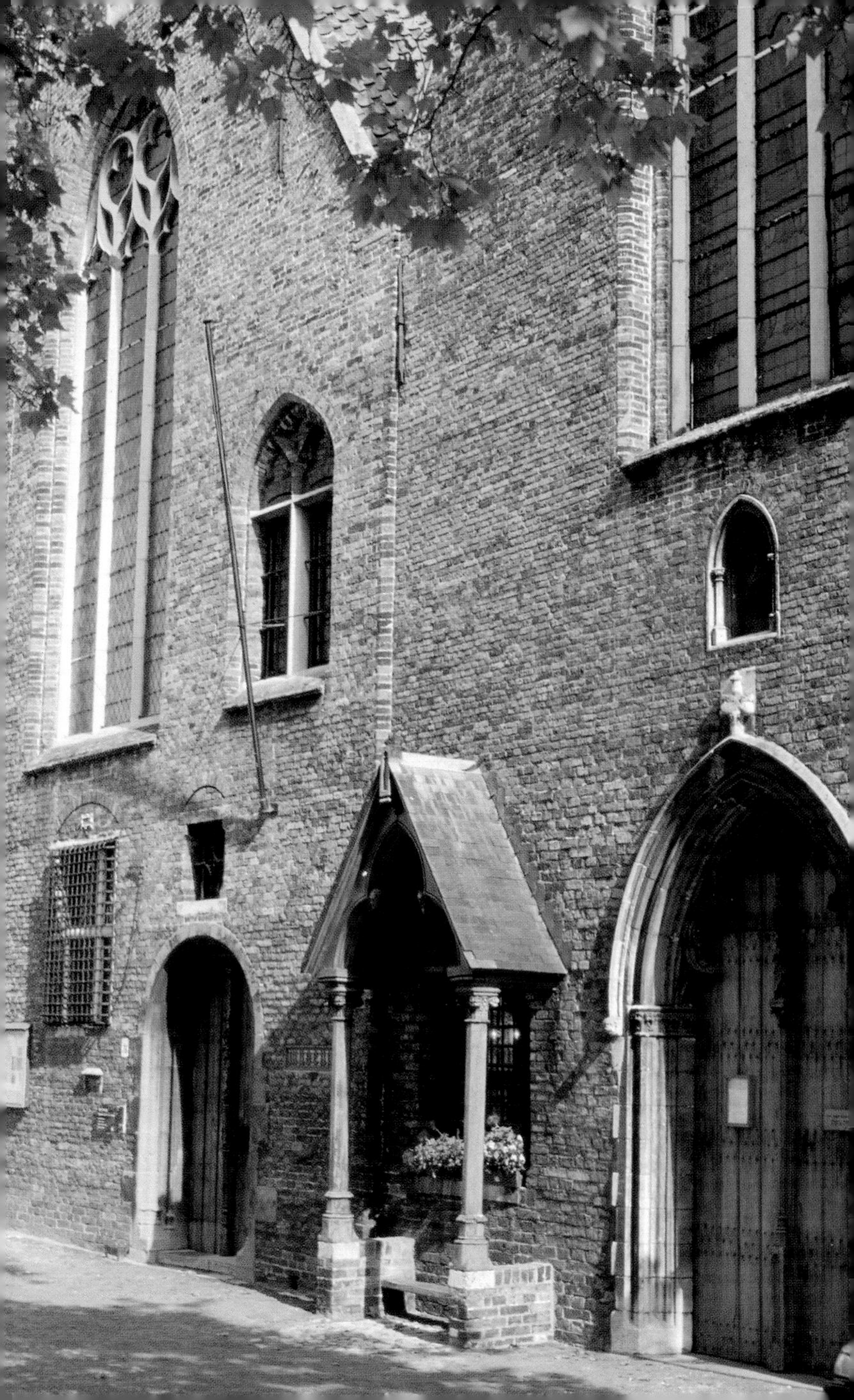

ing souvenirs of their visit to the guild. Since the time of Charles II, six kings and queens have signed the guild's visitors book.

Carmersstraat joins Kruisvest a short distance to the east, and, immediately right, perched on the grass-covered rampart, is **Sint Janshuysmolen**, a stilt windmill built to replace an earlier version on the same site, which blew down in 1744. Sint Janshuysmolen ceased operation in 1914, but was restored to working order in 1964, and is now the only functioning example in Bruges, where there were once twenty, all sited on the ramparts to take full advantage of any wind.

A miller, employed by the Bruges municipal authority, operates the windmill in the season — but a minimum three to four force wind is needed to set the sails in motion. Bear in mind that the wooden steps to the entrance are very steep and not suitable for young children or the infirm.

From the rampart looking southward may be seen the non-operational mill, Bonne Chiere, already referred to. It is in fact possible to take a photograph that incorporates both mills from the green facing Carmersstraat.

Northward from Carmersstraat the road becomes Peterseliestraat, a fairly lengthy stretch. Windmill adicts may wish to turn right at Leestenburg, continuing to Oostproostse, ahead, behind which, again on the rampart, stands **De Nieuwe Papegaai windmill**, brought to Bruges in 1970, but not in working order.

Peterseliestraat terminates at Potterierei. Immediately left, overlooking the canal, is one of the city's best-known establishments — take a deep breath — **Onze-Lieve-Vrouw ter Potterie** (Our Lady of the Pottery), a medieval hospice for elderly ladies. Facing the canal are seven dwellings built for them; each is gabled, thus earning the foundation its name The Seven Gifts of The Holy Spirit. These are followed by three much higher gables of: the former ward of the hospice, built in 1529; the hospital church of 1359; and the Lady Chapel, added to the church as a south aisle in 1625.

Records suggest that the hospice was established some time before 1276, but neither the precise date nor the name of the founder are known. It is certain, however, that an ancient pottery had once occupied the site, which is the reason, of course, for the hospital's strange name. In 1289, permission was given to build a church, no trace of which has survived. The foundation amalgamated around1300 with a similar hospice in Goezeputstraat. As was usual in the medieval period, not only was accommodation provided for the sick, but for travellers as well. Apart from the three ancient buildings, the hospital is now a retirement home for men and women, run by the state. Before entering, at number 79, ob-

Preceding page: Built as a medieval hospital, the ancient buildings of Onze-Lieve-Vrouw ter Potterie now form a museum

serve the Gothic chimney of the former sick ward, which is visible from the street.

Seen first is the entrance hall, created by partitioning the former sick ward. Display panels trace the detailed history of the hospital in Dutch, but translations are provided at reception. The hospital's collection of silver, paintings and sculpture is displayed throughout the hall and the old ward; most exhibits, however, are sixteenth or seventeenth-century work, not the greatest artistic period in Bruges.

After the Lady Chapel had been added to the church in 1625, thus forming a south aisle, the interior of the former was remodelled in Flemish Baroque style for the sake of unity; a Renaissance influence still being apparent. Inset on either side of the high altar are the tombs, left, of a hospice tutor, De Beer (died 1610) and his wife and, right, historian Nicolas Despars (died 1597).

Blocked arches on the north wall are a reminder that the church was originally open to the sick ward (prior, of course, to the creation of the hall). Separating the nave from the chancel, the rood screen is one of the most splendid in Bruges.

On the south wall of the Lady Chapel is a fine *Madonna of the Pevelenberg*, carved in the fourteenth century (but painted in 1920). Another Madonna with Child, the *Miraculous Statue of Our Lady of the Pottery*, also fourteenth-century work, stands on the marble altar.

The neo-Gothic tomb of St Idesbald, a Cistercian abbot of the nearby Ter Duinen Abbey (seen after leaving the hospital) is late nineteenth-century work.

Saint Idesbald (1100-1167), a Cistercian abbot of the foundation of Our Lady of the Dunes, lies in the tomb chest in the vestry on the south side of the Lady Chapel. The abbey was originally situated at Dunkirk, but its name Ter Duinen (of the Dunes) was kept when it transferred to Bruges, south of the hospital. The present tomb of the saint is relatively modern neo-Gothic work.

From the hospital, follow Potterierei southward, passing what, in medieval times, was the site of a shipbuilders yard. In contrast to the other buildings of Potterierei, which are relatively small, the **Episcopal Seminary**, at number 72, is enormous. Built around a green, with its church at the north end, the building originally formed a Cistercian Abbey, known as Ter Duinen (of the Dunes — a reference to its coastal foundation). In 1834, the buildings were taken over by the Bishop of Bruges, and the Episcopal Seminary was installed; the present church, built in 1788, was soon given the present Baroque-style gable to its canal frontage.

Permission to view must be obtained from the house at the south end of the complex, but few will find the church of great interest. The Seminary is built around a great courtyard, and the church is entered from the north-west corner of its enclosed, cloistered passage, the walls of which display large paintings, mostly portraits. Apart from a canopied Grecian structure behind the altar, and carved misericord stalls, the interior is rather plain.

Immediately south of the seminary is the picturesque **Duinenbrug**, which, although not ancient, is a rare Bruges example of a wooden bridge that can be raised and lowered to allow craft to pass. Cross the next bridge, Snaggaardsbrug to Langerei, left. First left, Sint Gilliskoorstraat provides a splendid view of Sint Gilliskerk ahead.

Sint Gilliskerk (St Giles Church) is entered from its west end between 3pm and 6pm only. It was begun in 1240, but no Romanesque features appear to have survived externally, primarily because aisles were added between 1462 and 1479, both of them the same height as the existing nave. The nave and chancel, however, retain a Romanesque barrel vault of timber, the only example in Bruges to survive. All structural work is of brick, apart from the two piers of the nave, which are built of stone.

The history of the Trinitarian brotherhood is related in four works by the Brugean artist Jan Garemijn, which are the only paintings of importance in the church.

A memorial erected in 1994 commemorates Hans Memling; the great painter, who was buried in Sint Gilliskerk in 1561; although his grave has never been discovered. It is also known that the painter Lanceloot Blondeel was buried in the church in 1561, however, his grave and tombstone have similarly been lost. Sint Gilliskerk possesses two organs, the oldest of them, in the gallery of the church's north aisle, and a modern instrument in the south aisle, which is played in the organ competition that forms part of the Flanders Fair.

Running southward from the church is Sint Gilliskerkstraat. The painter Jan van Eyck lived at 6 Gouden Handstraat, left. This leads to Gouden Handbrug, right, and is immediately followed by another bridge, left, at right angles to it, Carmersbrug. Cross this to Sint Annarei, first right, and turn first left along Blekersstraat where, at number 2, is **Vlissinghe**, one of the most famous taverns in Bruges (open after 2pm but not Mondays).

Vlissinghe is reputed to have opened as a café in 1515, but not under its present name. Although some of the decor is seventeenth century, a great deal of kitsch has been added recently — not to everyone's approval. Locals still frequent the tavern and don't seem to object to tourists drinking in their 'local'.

Return to Sint Annarei and cross Strobrug, the bridge immediately ahead, to Spinolarei. Koningstraat, first left, leads to Sint Walburgakerk, which faces Sint Maartensplein.

Although **Sint Walburgakerk** (St Walburga Church) is only open half an hour before services, or 6-10pm July, August and September, it is usually possible to view the interior

Following page: Reminiscent of Amsterdam, Duinenbrug is a survival of the drawbridges which were once common in Bruges

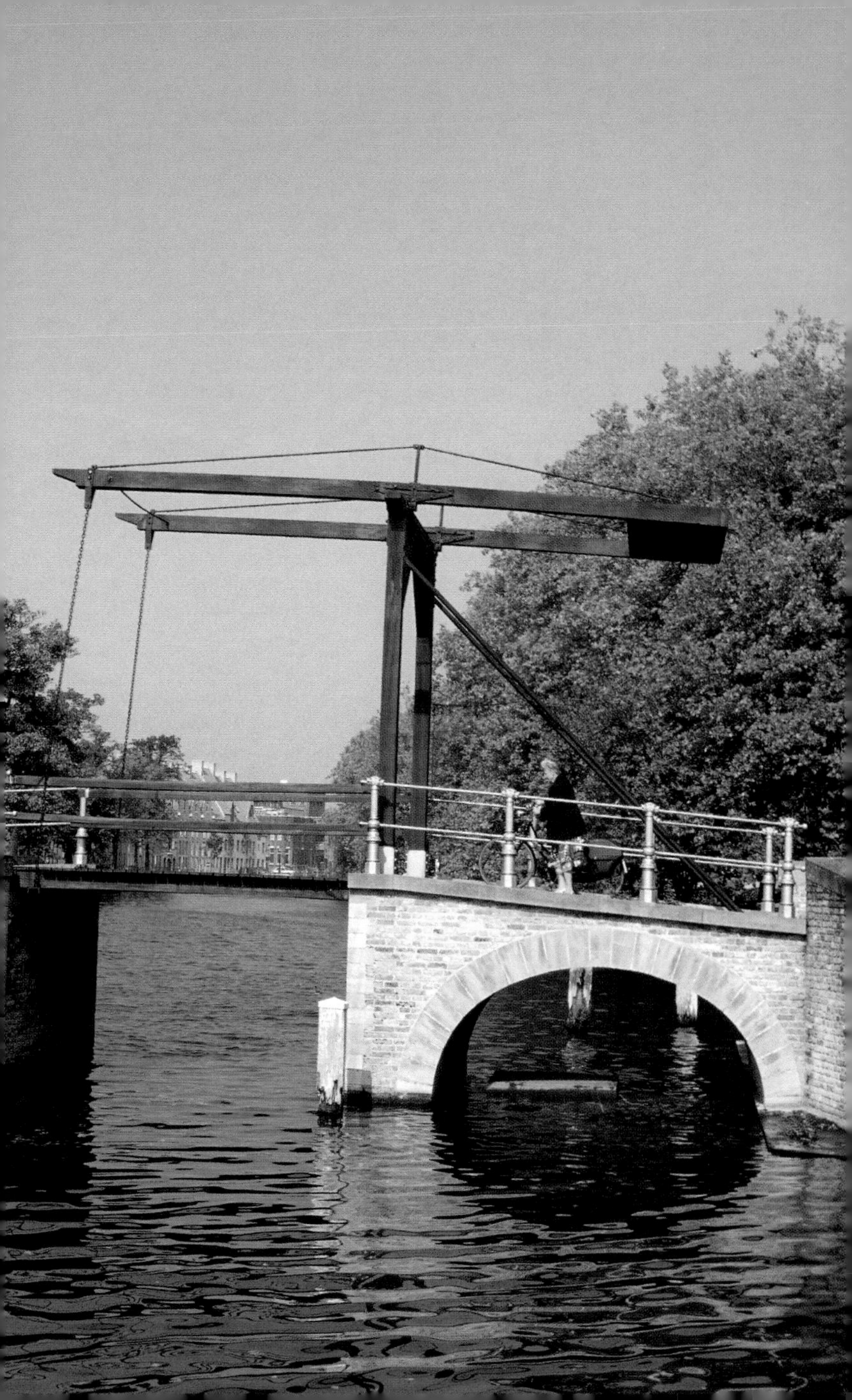

through its glass inner door. Consecrated in 1641, as was usual in Jesuit churches, this example was modelled on Il Gesù, in Rome, the first church built for that Order. Its architect was a Jesuit brother, Pieter Huyssens, the son of a mason, who designed similar churches in Ghent and Antwerp. During the French Revolution, Sint Walburgakerk became a Temple of Law, but reopened for Catholic worship once more in 1804.

The Baroque interior is remarkable for its sumptuous furnishings and fittings. Worth a visit on its own account is the pulpit carved of wood in 1669 by Artus Quellinus (or Quellin), reputedly the master from whom England's Grinling Gibbon learnt his craft. Quellinus spent a great deal of time sculpting the marble interior of the Royal Palace in Amsterdam and, in consequence, examples of his work are too rarely seen elsewhere. Few pulpits equal Sint Walburga's in dramatic power — a preacher hardly seems to be needed! Particularly striking is the canopy, which appears to be swept by a powerful wind. Looking up to the pulpit from the floor of the church it is difficult to avoid the searching gaze of the cherubs.

On leaving Sint Walburgakerk, turn left and follow Sint Maartensplein to Boomgaardstraat, which leads to Hoogstraat, right.

The **Aarendshuis Hotel**, 18-20 Hoogstraat, rather ambitiously claims that Napoleon and Josephine stayed in one of their rooms in 1811. This is somewhat surprising, as Napoleon disposed of Josephine in January 1810, when he arranged the annulment of their marriage. In addition, although they certainly visited Bruges, it is recorded that the couple slept on that occasion in Sluis (Holland). A three star hotel, there is some Empire-style décor, and six of the rooms have four-poster beds.

On the same side of the road, at number 6, is the rather grim and apparently derelict **Huis de Zeven Toren** (House of Seven Towers). Only at basement level are there traces of the original stone mansion built for Bonin van den Gapere in 1320. The mansion's distinguishing feature was seven slender towers protruding above the roofline, hence its name, but these were demolished in 1717. King Charles II of England lived here during his exile in Bruges during Cromwell's Commonwealth. In return for the city's hospitality, Charles gave permission for 50 vessels from Bruges to fish in English waters.

Diligence Bar, almost opposite, at number 5, serves some of the most economically-priced beer in central Bruges; and there is a friendly bar at which to sit. Genuine Trappist beer is available bottled or draught.

Hoogstraat leads to Markt via Burg.

Additional Information

Places to Visit

Engels Klooster (English Convent)
85 Carmersstraat
Open: 2-4pm, 4.30-5.30pm. Closed every 1st Sunday (except on Church holidays).

Gouden Boom (De) Brewery Visit
Langestraat
Groups (minimum 15 persons)
150 BF per person. Includes 1 drink.
Only on request.
(☎ 050 33 06 99)

Gouden Boom (De) Museum
10 Verbrand Nieuwland
Open: 1 June-30 September, Wednesday-Sunday 2-5pm.

Guido Gezellemuseum (Gezelle Museum)
64 Rolweg
Open: 1 April-30 September 9.30am-12noon, 12.45-5pm.
1 October-31 March 9.30am-12.30pm, 2-5pm. Closed Tuesday.

Kantcentrum (Lace Centre)
3A Peperstraat
Open: 1 April-30 September 10am-12noon, 2-6pm. 1 October-31 March 10am-12noon, 2-5pm. Closed on Sunday. Demonstrations every afternoon.

Museum voor Volkskunde (Folklore Museum)
40 Rolweg
Open: 1 April-30 September 9.30am-5pm. 1 October-31 March 9.30am-12.30pm, 2-5pm. Closed Tuesday.

Onze-Lieve-Vrouw ter Potterie (Museum)
79 Potterierei
Open: 1 April-30 September 9.30am-12noon, 12.45-5pm.
1 October-31 March 9.30am-12.30pm, 2-5pm.
Closed Wednesday.

Sint Janshuysmolen (Windmill)
Kruisvest
Open: 1 May-30 September 9.30am-12noon, 12.45-5pm (depending on wind).

Sint Jorisgilde (Guild of St George)
59 Stijn Streuvelsstraat
Open: 2-6pm (closed Wednesday, Saturday and Sunday). Saturday: only groups (on request).

Sint Sebastiaansgilde (Guild of St Sebastian)
174 Carmersstraat
Open: Monday, Wednesday, Friday and Saturday 10am-12noon, 2-5pm.

North Bruges

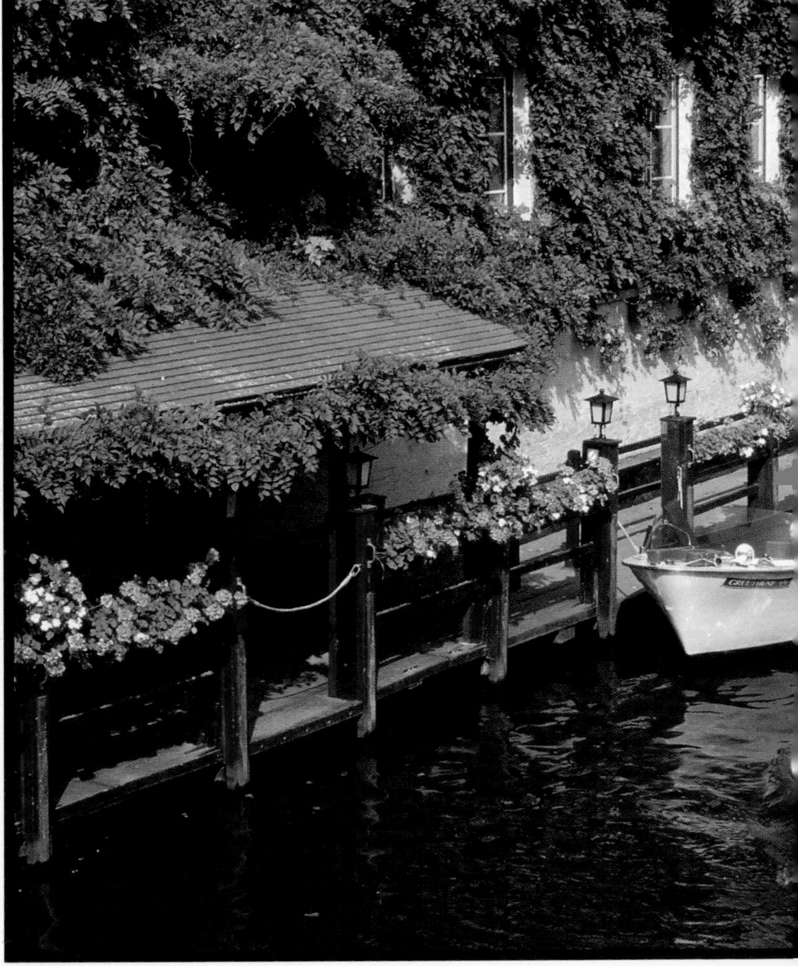

3

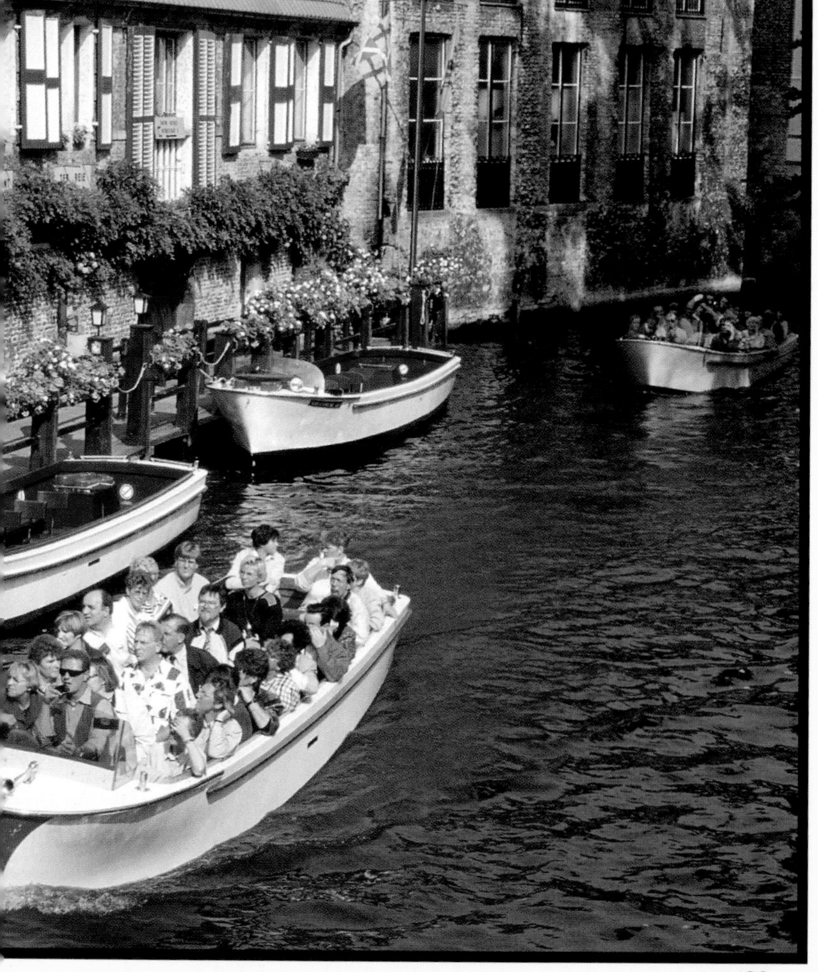

Tranquil Canals and Medieval Trading Houses

Beginning and ending at **Markt**, fine weather is needed for this itinerary, as St James's Church (Sint Jakobskerk) is the only building that can be entered. Many of the canal stretches passed will have few visitors, and their relative solitude gives an 'Old Bruges' atmosphere that is unmatched by the more popular waterways.

Sint Amandsstraat, which leads westward from Markt, is a lively street, most of its cafés and taverns having outdoor terraces. Very soon, the thoroughfare opens up to form a small square, which was created in 1817 when the Sint Amandskapel was demolished. Its place was taken by the huge water pump, a contemporary of the similar pump in Vismarkt.

In the Middle Ages, Sint Amandsstraat formed part of the route taken by state processions from Sint Donaas cathedral, in Burg, to the Prinsenhof palace. Only traces of Prinsenhof have survived, incorporated in the present nineteenth-century structure built in the square called Prinsenhof, which is visited later. Sint Amandsstraat ends at the Noordzandstraat/Geldmuntstraat junction, immediately north of which lies Muntplein. The names of both Geldmuntstraat and Muntplein commemorate the building in which coins were minted around 1300 to 1786; it stood in the adjacent Gheerwijnstraat, but no longer survives.

An equestrian statue of Mary of Burgundy 'Flandria Nostra' stands in Muntplein; it is the work of Jules Lagae, 1987. Return to Geldmuntstraat, right, first left Prinsenhof.

Philip the Good expanded the residence of the counts in Noordzandstraat by adding further courtyards, and the complex, finished in 1429, was named **Prinsenhof**. The previous year, Philip, in search of a third wife, commissioned Jan van Eyck to paint a portrait of the eminently suitable Isabella, daughter of the king of Portugal, to see if he approved of her looks. He did, and the marriage took place in 1430, the wedding feast at Prinsenhof being one of the greatest celebrations in the history of the city. During the ceremony, Philip founded the Order of the Golden Fleece. Although a lamb's fleece appears to be the source of the Order's name, it has been alleged that the golden hair of Maria Crombrugghe, a Bruges beauty, was the true inspiration. Others see a connection with the Greek legend of Jason and the Golden Fleece. It is said that fourteen ships brought the wedding guests to Bruges, all of them disembarking at the north end of Minnewater.

Philip's son, Charles the Bold, held an even more splendid wedding feast at Prinsenhof in 1468, following his marriage to Margaret of

Preceding pages: There are many embarkation points in Bruges for the half-hour-long boat trips on the canals; all follow the same route

York, Edward IV's sister. Like his father, the Duke was making a third trip to the altar, but no expense was spared. Burgundian wine flowed from the public water fountains in the streets.

Served at the feast was an immense pastry, which concealed an entire orchestra. A further surprise for the wedding guests was an artificial whale, from within which forty choristers sang.

One of the guests thus entertained was William Caxton, who would later print *The Recuyall of the History of Troy*, at Bruges in 1475, the first book to be printed in the English language. Caxton's task in Bruges at the time, however, was to represent, as governor, the English merchants operating throughout the Burgundian Netherlands. Seeing the enormous potential for printing in England Caxton returned to his homeland in 1476, and set up a printing press in Westminster Abbey.

In 1958, it was decided to commemorate the great ceremony every 5 years in August. Known as the Pageant of the Golden Tree, a procession with two thousand participants dressed in fifteenth-century Burgundian costumes parades through the city streets. The history of Flanders, Bruges in particular, is depicted in various set pieces,the high spot being the arrival of 'Charles and Margaret' at Bruges.

Those who have visited Onze-Lieve-Vrouwekerk may already have seen the tomb of Charles the Bold and his daughter Mary of Burgundy. Mary gave birth to Philip the Fair at the Prinsenhof in 1479, only to die there 3 years later following a hunting accident. After her death, the dukedom of Burgundy came to an end, and much of Prinsenhof, by then little used, was sold. From 1622, English Franciscan nuns operated a boarding school for the daughters of wealthy English Catholics in its few remaining buildings. Entirely disposed of by French revolutionaries in 1794, a Boulogne monastery eventually took over the site, building a new Prinsenhof in neo-Gothic style; some of the ancient fabric was apparently incorporated in the structure. Prinsenhof may not be visited, unless to attend a concert, exhibition or conference, which are occasionally held within.

Undoubtedly the original Prinsenhof would have incorporated superb architecture, and it is with a sense of loss that the rather unprepossessing square that bears its name is left. From the south-west corner of Prinsenhof, Ontvangerstraat leads northward to Moerstraat, right. After the Gheerwijnstraat/Leeuwstraat crossing, Moerstraat opens out to form Sint Jakobsplein, in which stands Sint Jakobskerk.

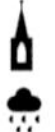

Sint Jakobskerk (St James's Church) was founded in 1240 as a small chapel. Rich merchants in the locality gave their support, and the building was greatly enlarged in the fifteenth century by the addition of late-Gothic aisles.

Internally, like so many Bruges churches, Sint Jakob has been remodelled in Baroque style. Its pa-

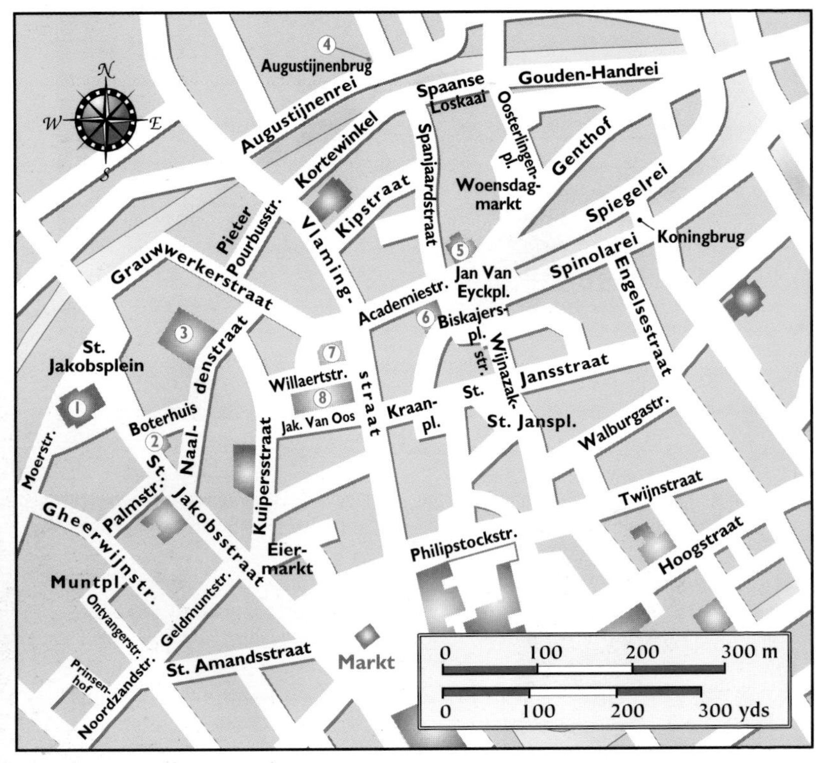

KEY

1. St James's Church (Sint Jakobskerk)
2. Boterhuis (theatre)
3. Bladelin Court (Hof Bladelin)
4. Augustijnenbrug
5. Customs House (Tolhuis)
6. Burgher's Lodge (Poortersloge)
7. House of the Genoese (Saaihalle) and Huize ter Beurze
8. City Theatre (Stadsschouwburg)

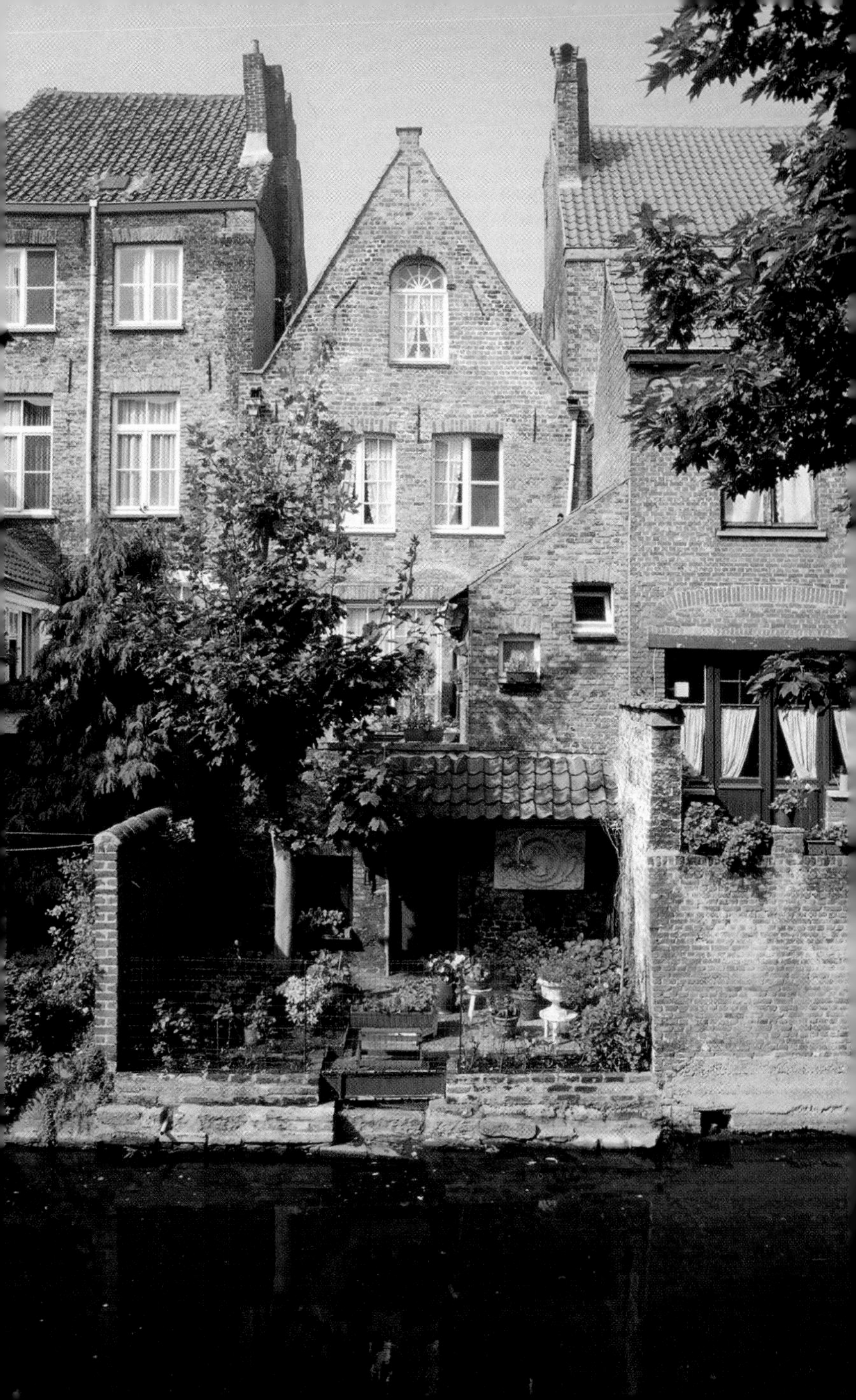

trons included the Duke of Burgundy and the wealthy Portinari, De Gros and Moreel families, with the result that an unusual number of paintings was purchased, almost giving the impression of an art gallery. The most important of these, one of the best known Flemish Primitive works, dominates the chapel in the north aisle of the nave: *The Legend of St Lucy* triptych, painted in 1480 by an unknown artist, who is known simply as the 'Master of the Legend of St Lucy'. Its caption, in Dutch, reads *De legende van de H. Lucia de meester van de Lucia legende 1480*. Lucy, obviously an extremely charitable lady, is shown giving all her belongings to the poor; she is then accused of being a Christian by her fiancé, who has seen Lucy dispose of her dowry, and found guilty, being condemned to work in a brothel; but even with the help of two oxen, the brothel owners are unable to drag Lucy away with them. Although the story is set in Syracuse, the background to the third panel is obviously Bruges — the lantern has not yet been added to the belfry.

The last chapel of the chancel's south aisle is generally regarded as the finest in Bruges. Late-Gothic in style, it was commissioned by Ferry De Gros, Treasurer of the Order of the Golden Fleece, who died in 1544. Forming the top section of a two-tier layout is the joint tomb of De Gros and his first wife, which was probably made in 1521, the year of her death. Their recumbent effigies surmount the tomb. Forming the lower tier, and also surmounted by a recumbent effigy, is the tomb of the second wife of De Gros, who died in 1530. Above the chapel's altar is a terracotta Virgin and Child medallion, in the Renaissance style of the Italian Della Robbia family. Ceramic tiles, contemporary with it, surround the altar.

A splendid brass memorial of 1577, commemorating a Spanish merchant, Francisco de Lapuebla and his wife, embellishes the chapel of the nave's south aisle.

Opposite the north side of the church, from 16 Moerstraat, runs a cobbled lane, approached through double gates, which are unlocked during the day. It passes, on the right, a row of almshouses identified as **Vette Vischpoort 1434**. At the end of the narrow lane flows a canal, which is overlooked on its opposite bank by a delightful, flower-bedecked house, the sudden, theatrical appearance of which is quite startling.

Return to Sint Jakobskerkplein and proceed to the east side. Facing the chancel of the church is an ancient example of a red pillar box, apparently still used for letters.

Follow Sint Jakobsstraat from the south-east corner of the square, noting a range of ten step gabled houses on the north side, **numbers 38-56**. On the opposite side, at 41, the **Hotel**

Preceding page: Approached from a narrow lane off Moerstraat, this canal view is a visual surprise

Navarra was the mansion of Juan de Peralta, who acted as consul for the Spanish merchants of Navarre in the seventeenth century.

Boterhuis, at number 36, was originally a building used by the dairy trade, which operated here from the late sixteenth century until around 1860, when the building became a concert hall; it now accommodates a café and a theatre, Theater de Korre. The present Classical façade was constructed in 1830.

Boterhuis (the street) leads eastward from beside the building, and incorporates the small square in which milk and butter (but not eggs) were once sold.

Naaldenstraat, first left, boasts two historic buildings. At its south end, on the west side, stood **Hof van Gistel**, in 1444 the mansion of Antoine de Bourbon, Duke of Vendôme, and later the residence of Jean de Matance of Burgos, leader of the important Spanish trading community in Bruges. All that survives is its circular tower, which is best seen from the north end of Naaldenstraat, where, at number 19, Hof Bladelin has survived in its entirety.

To enter **Hof Bladelin**, ring the bell to the right of the doorway, which will then click open. Turn immediately right and ask the attendant (who probably will not speak English) for the archivist, and wait for her to arrive. At the time of writing, Sister Claeys conducted visitors around the courtyard.

Pieter Bladelin, councillor of Philip the Good and Treasurer of the Order of the Golden Fleece, built the east (entrance) range of the mansion and most of the south range, including its tower, around 1440. Original stone corbels support the vault of the arcade to the house. That left of its door depicts a woman with her dog, representing fidelity. The other shows St Alphege of Canterbury holding a bone; he was allegedly martyred in 1012 by drunken Danes, who battered him with animal bones after he had refused to pay a ransom demand.

Piero de Medici, of the Florentine banking family, bought the property in 1466, adding a banking room to the west of Bladelin's range — the join can just be seen externally. In 1473, the entrepreneurial Medici representative in Bruges, Tomaso Portinari, resided in the house and was painted by Memling.

Externally, the Medicis left their mark primarily on the arcade fronting the exit. Embedded in its courtyard wall are two Renaissance medallions dating from around 1473 depicting busts of Piero's son Lorenzo the Magnificent and his wife Clarice Orsini.

Within the arcade, corbels are carved with the Medici family emblem of three peacock feathers within a ring. On the bosses of the vault, similar feathers encircle seven red orbs, which signify Piero de Medici. Lorenzo the Magnificent was represented by eight orbs, whilst six orbs signified his grandfather Cosimo — the mathematical logic of a family of bankers!

The range facing the house was built in 1568, replacing a building

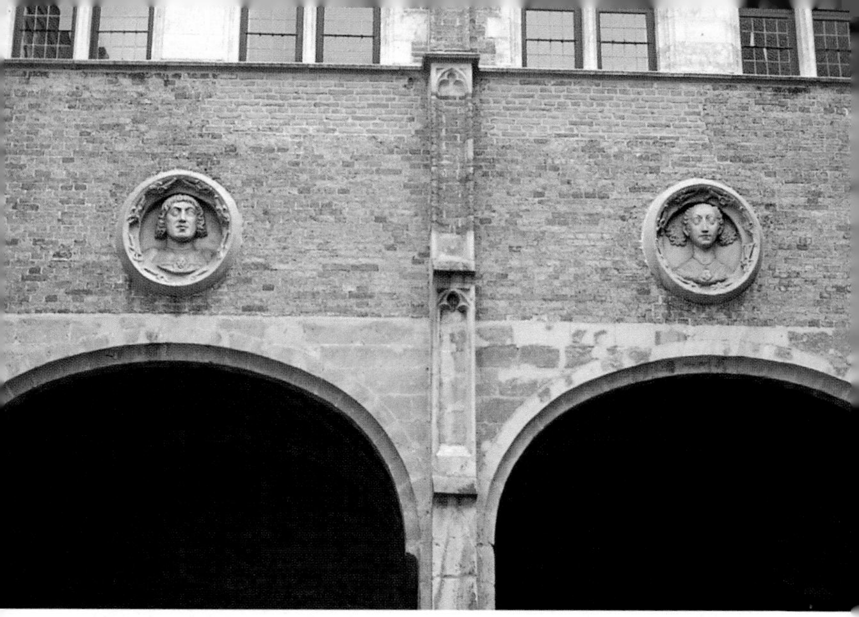

Overlooking the medieval courtyard of Hof Bladelin, Renaissance medallions were added during the Medici period of occupancy

The romantic way to see Bruges

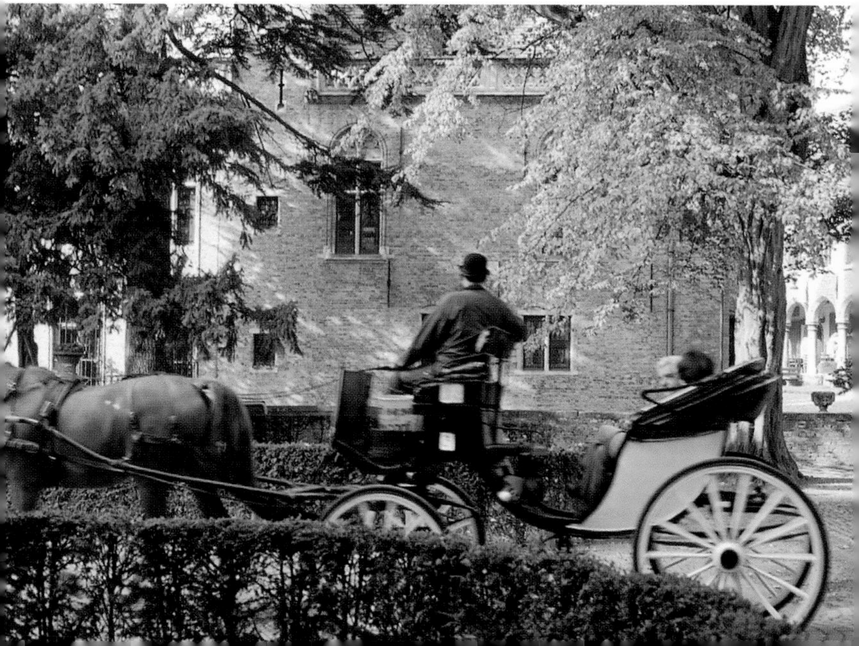

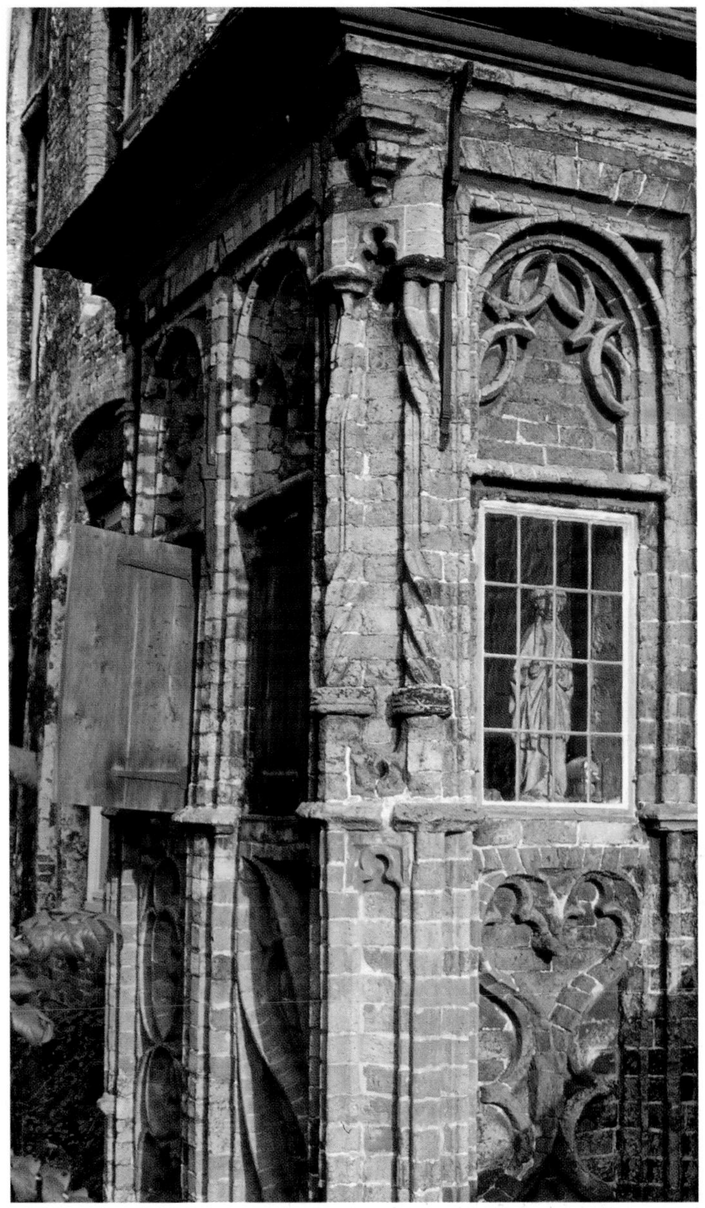

which, Bladelin apparently kept after he had disposed of the remainder. Finally, the west range, which leads to the garden, was added in 1623, thus enclosing the courtyard.

From the delightful rear garden, there are still traces of a second tower that Bladelin had built. Presumably, this was removed by the Medicis when they built their banking hall. Margaret von Vageriere lived in a house on the south side of Bladelin's estate before her marriage to Bladelin.

If convenient, some lucky visitors may be shown the interior of the banking hall and Bladelin's salon. The hall combines Medici and Burgundian symbols. Repetition of the peacock feathers and orbs already seen will be noted on the beams and corbels. Burgundian mottos *Semper* (always) and *Mon Joie* (My Pleasure), their battle-cry, may have been later additions. The fireplace is original.

Bladelin's salon, reached from the hall, is decorated with paintings by a pupil of Raphael, 1521; they were not acquired until the Medicis had vacated the house. The arms of Philip the Good and Isabella of Portugal decorate the room. Count Egmont (immortalised by Beethoven in his Overture to Goethe's play) lived here briefly in the sixteenth century. He was accused of treason by the Duke of Alba and executed in Brussels.

Facing the street, above the entrance to Hof Bladelin, the polychrome sculpture depicts Bladelin kneeling before the Virgin; it is late nineteenth-century neo-Gothic work by our old friend Louis Delacenserie who, no doubt, would have loved to 'improve' the entire house.

Opposite Hof Bladelin, **Hotel Lucca**, originally the trading house of Italian merchants from Lucca, retains a fourteenth-century cellar, now converted to the reception area and a bar. It is believed that bales of silk were kept there.

Follow Naaldenstraat southward to Sint Jakobsstraat where, immediately opposite, is the **Stedelijk Conservatorium** (City Music School). Towards Markt, **In den Wittenkop** offers good bar food, and opposite, at number 13, **Pietje Pek** specialises in international dishes and an amusing display of menus.

Eiermarkt (Egg Market) is a small but lively square interupting Sint Jakobsstraat just before Markt is reached. Most of its buildings now accommodate bars and restaurants, which are extremely popular — and crowded at weekends. **D'Eiermarkt** specializes in Flemish dishes — and will even serve boiled potatoes rather than chips when not too busy. At number 9, **'t Voske Malpertuus** boasts a restaurant with a sixteenth-century monastic cellar. Its speciality is a massive *waterzooi* fish stew — rich, creamy and served as two helpings. **Raadskelder**, nearby, is recommended for mussels.

Preceding page: Brick cannot be carved, but the medieval craftsmen of Bruges were able to make it appear that it could. This oriel window beside Vlamingbrug overlooks Augustijnenrei

Some will have observed that Belgians do not eat cheese as part of a three or four course meal, as do their French neighbours: there are therefore few cheese specialist shops to be seen in Bruges. At number 2 Eiermarkt, however, **De Brugse Kaashoeve** is a rare example in the city. A wide range of French cheeses is stocked, but lovers of real stinkers — the type that as soon as you put your key in the front door rushes to greet you, carrying your carpet slippers — will wish to try Herve. Herve, in the form of a square block, is a Belgian cheese that is hardly ever found outside the country. It makes a ripe Camembert seem innocuous, and, in deference to those sensitive to powerful odours, should not be purchased until just before returning home. Those travelling by train accompanied by a Herve have a good chance of making the journey in an empty compartment.

A Baroque water fountain of stone survives in the square.

Head directly northward from Eiermarkt along Kuipersstraat, passing the city library, **De Biekorf**, left. At the street's north end, **'t Zwart Huis Taverne**, at 23, was built in 1480. Note the brick trefoil Gothic tracery in the niches above its windows.

Facing the tavern, Adriaan Willaertstraat leads to Vlamingstraat, left. On the left is **Stadsschouwberg**, the city's main theatre, erected in 1869. A statue of bird-catcher Papageno from Mozart's *The Magic Flute* stands in front of the building.

In the fifteenth century, this part of **Vlamingstraat** became the financial centre of Bruges. At that time, the north end of the thoroughfare narrowed to little more than an alleyway, and the square created was known as Beursplein (another Beursplein now exists to the south-west of Bruges, but it has no connection with this one).

Built as the Genoese Trading House in 1399, **Saaihalle** (Serge Hall), number 33 Vlamingstraat, is the only example of a medieval trading house in Bruges to survive, although much altered. In addition to importing the usual spices and precious stones and metals, the Genoese specialized in alum, from Asia Minor, which was used for fixing leather dyes. It will be noted immediately that the building is faced with a honey-coloured stone rather than the usual brick. This came from a small quarry near Ghent and was extremely expensive, indicative of the great wealth of the Genoese.

The late-Gothic entrance portal is original, including the relief in its tympanum of St George (patron saint of the Genoese) slaying the dragon. The narrow second door and window are twentieth-century additions to the rest of the ground floor, which originally comprised a bare wall apart from the entrance. The first floor is little altered. Originally, the upper storey was formed by a false, crenellated wall, with two large windows, but this was re-

Following page: Augustijnenrei is regarded as one of the most picturesque canal stretches in the city

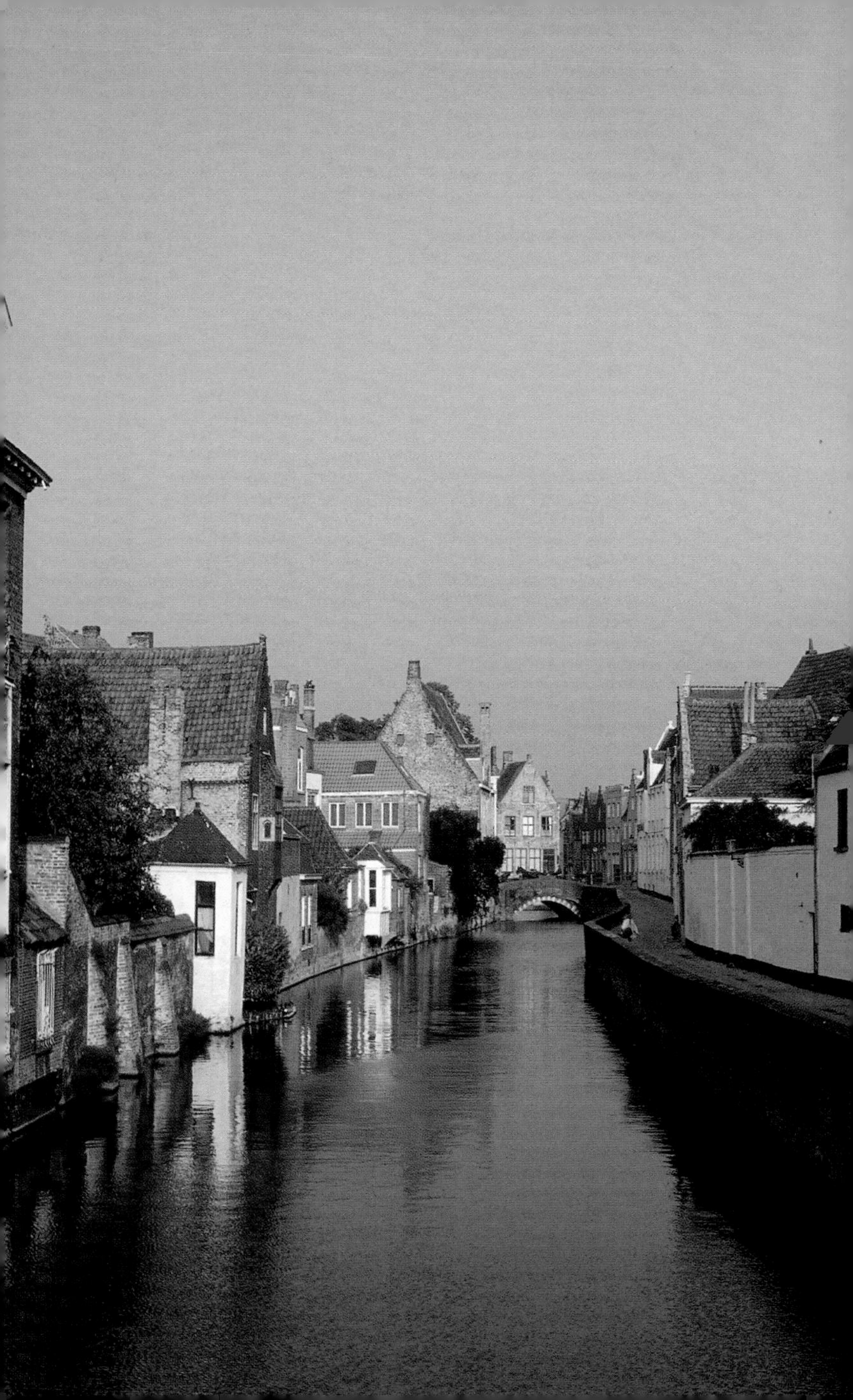

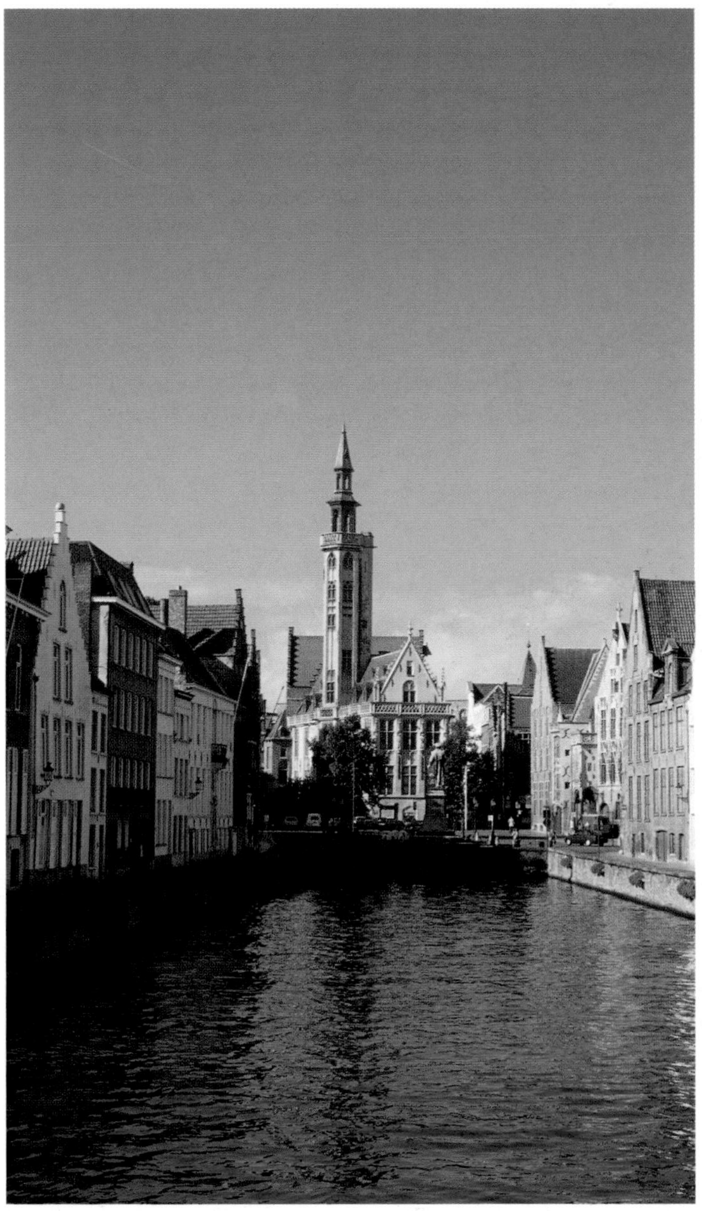

placed in 1720 by the present bell gable, a Dutch feature rarely seen in Bruges.

In 1516, the Genoese followed the trend by transferring to Antwerp, and the Serge Weavers took over the premises as their trade hall. The building's present name Saaihalle commemorates their occupancy.

Next door, at 35, **Huize ter Beurze** (House of the Bourse), built in 1453, has been faithfully restored to its original appearance by the bank that now owns it. A thirteenth-century inn formerly stood here under the sign of The Three Purses (*beurse* is Dutch for purse). Italian and Spanish merchants conducted their business in the tavern, and trading prices were posted outside, the name *beurse* soon becoming synonymous with stock dealing. The family that had owned the inn since 1276 changed their name to Van der Beurse, and stayed in residence after the present building was constructed, not vacating it until 1483. Meanwhile, their name had been adopted by leading European stock exchanges: *bourse* in France, *borsa* in Italy, *bolsa* in Spain, and *borse* in Germany; England, naturally, preferred to be different, calling their stock dealing centre simply The Exchange.

Beursplein became the Bruges base for Italian merchants; all of them were fierce competitors, and they probably built their trading houses close together so that they could keep an eye on each other. The house of the Venetians stood at the north end of Beursplein until it was demolished for the widening of Vlamingstraat in 1965.

On the Academiestraat corner opposite, the first building on the north side (**number 1**) occupies the former site of the Florentine trading hall, which was a most impressive building, with slender twin turrets. Now a shop, the plaque on its Vlamingstraat side wall quotes Dante's fourteenth-century disparaging reference, in *The Divine Comedy*, to the newly constructed Bruges-Wissamt dike. Dante studied in Paris and may have heard about the dike from fellow students, or even visited Bruges himself.

Continuing along Vlamingstraat, **number 51** is a late-Gothic house built for Jacob Cnoop, whose daughter married the painter Gerard David. The house, with an unusual roofline, was under restoration in 1995. Also late-Gothic is the building opposite, at 82, with a stone oriel window.

The most splendid oriel window in Bruges, however, is seen by continuing ahead to Vlamingbrug, and looking right from the bridge to the rear of **100 Vlamingstraat**. Overlooking the canal, its oriel window demonstrates how richly decorative Flemish brickwork could be. It was commissioned by Herman van Oudvelde, a goldsmith, in 1514. Recently discovered tiny chimneys in the roof of the oriel indicate that the area was

Preceding page: Poortersloge, formerly a meeting place for burghers, is distinguished by its slender tower, the most delicate in Bruges

used by the goldsmith for smelting.

Before crossing the bridge, some may wish to return to Vlamingstraat and explore Kortewinkel and Pieter Pourbusstraat which cross it a few paces to the south. Most of the houses in the two interconnecting streets are extremely ancient, with many examples of step gables, and even some rare timber façades.

The stone-built **Vlamingbrug** has low benches that were not seats but platforms on which merchants displayed their wares. On the opposite side of the canal **Augustijnenrei** snakes eastward, affording some of the most tranquil scenery in Bruges.

Now supporting a garden on the opposite (south) side of the canal, the curved brick arches are a fragment of the second enclosing city rampart that was built, together with the canal, in 1127. **Augustijnenbrug**, the next bridge, built in 1391, also of stone, is supposed to be the city's oldest bridge to survive. It was constructed to provide friars with a short cut from their Augustinian monastery to the city centre. More benches for merchants are similar to those seen on Vlamingbrug.

Cross Augustijnenbrug to Spaanse Loskaai, left, its name announcing that we have entered the former trading quarter of the Spanish merchants.

From Spaanse Loskaai, on the opposite side of the canal can be seen **Hotel Ter Brughe**, the most photographed of the city's ancient hotels.

A right turn conducts the visitor into the rectangular square known as Oosterlingenplein, and a rapid transition from Spanish to German Bruges has now been made. Oosterlingen literally means Men from the East, as Germans were referred to. At number 1, next to Hotel Bryghia, stands what remains of **Oosterlingenhuis** the former Trading House of the Hanseatic League. Their house in Bruges had been founded at a great ceremony attended by an august collection of mayors from four of the League's member cities: Bremen, Cologne, Hamburg and Lubeck. Only the lower sections of the original Oosterlingenhuis, designed for the League by local architect Jan van der Poele in 1478, have survived. The present building has a similar crenellated roof to that illustrated in a seventeenth-century print of the building. Above the entrance is the double-headed eagle emblem of the League.

The Germans shipped fur, grain, beer and wine to the city, but unlike their Spanish and British neighbours, never built their own weigh-house. Boycotted economically, the Hanseatic League members were among the first to move to Antwerp.

Oosterlingenplein merges with Woensdagmarkt, the Wednesday market of its name recently transferring from Burg to Markt. The central figure of Hans **Memling Statue** erected in 1874.

Following page: A rare example of stonework in Bruges, Tolhuis was the point from where excise duties were collected on all goods being shipped inland. Attached to it, left, is the former guildhouse of the Stevedores, one of the narrowest façades in the city

---

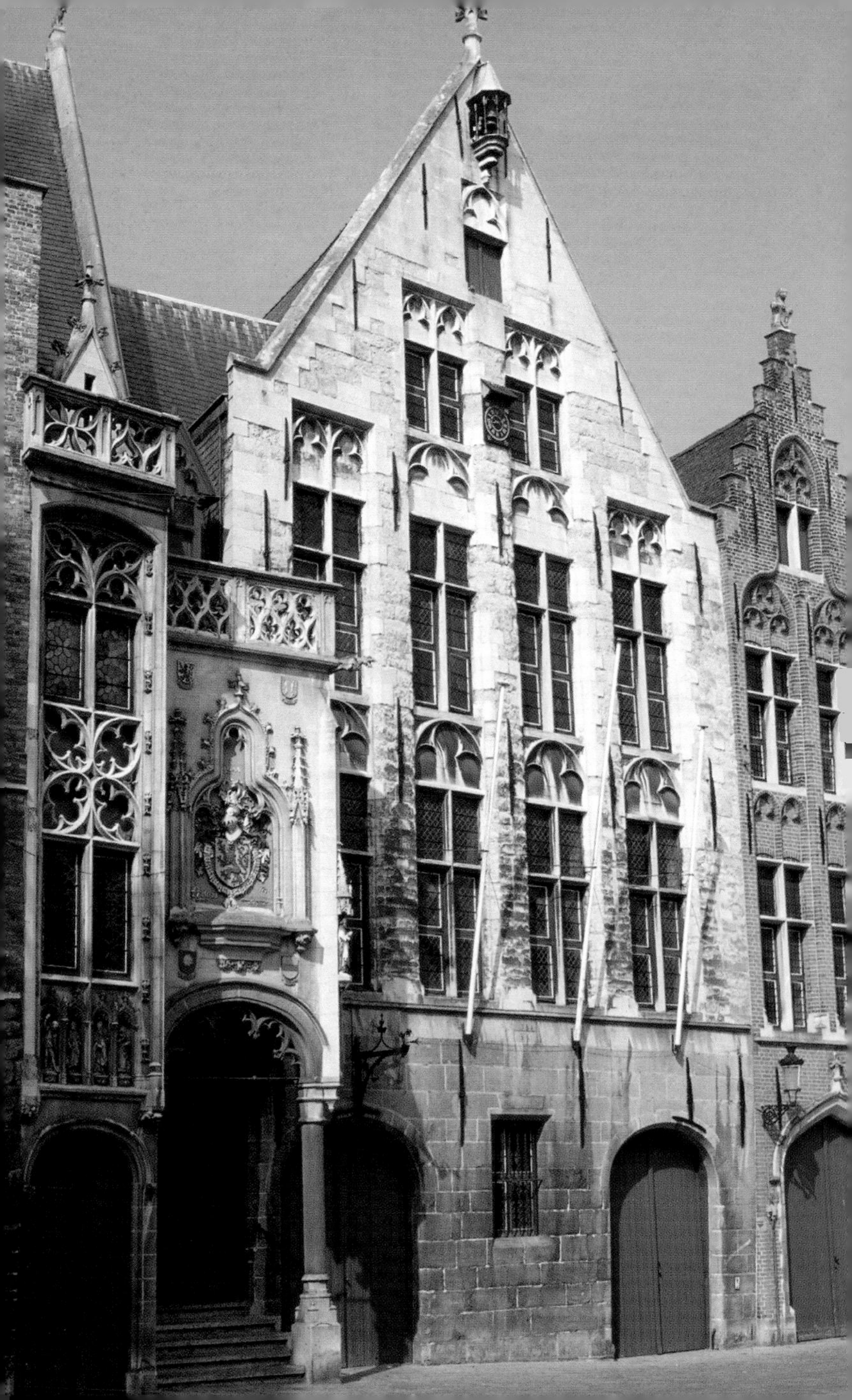

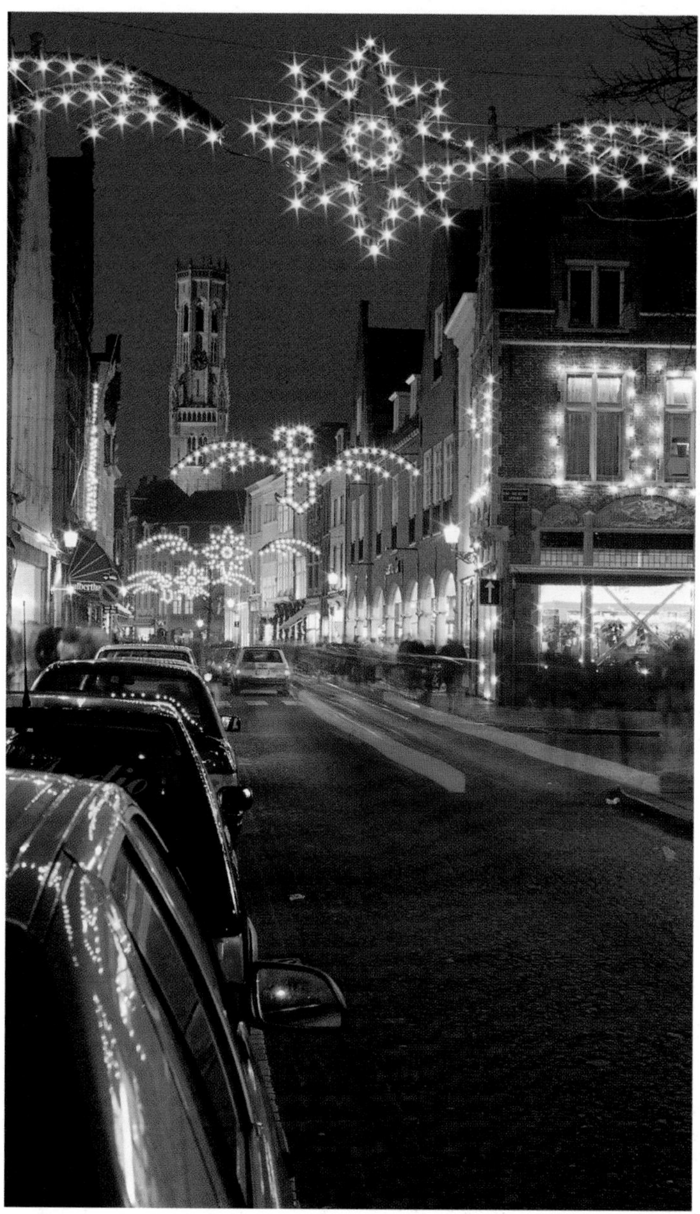

To the south, **Jan Van Eyckplein** is one of the most picturesque squares in Bruges. Its **Van Eyck statue** is the late-nineteenth-century work of the same sculptor responsible for the slightly earlier figure of Memling just seen.

On the north side of the square, **Tolhuis** (Customs House) was rebuilt in 1478 for Pieter of Luxembourg, whose gilded coat of arms is carved above the entrance. Through inheritance he acquired the personal right to levy customs duty on goods shipped inland from Bruges; this duty remained in force until the late eighteenth century, and its collectors lived here. Formerly, the canal came right up to the building, and goods were unloaded at Sint Jansbrug, the bridge that faced it but which no longer exists as the water has been filled in.

Immediately left is an unusually narrow building, the former **Huis der Lastdragers**, guildhouse of the Stevedores. Built in 1470, its Flamboyant tracery is typical of Brabantine Gothic of the late fifteenth century. Note the heads of dockers carved on the corbels.

Dominating Jan Van Eyckplein, however, is **Poortersloge**, at 14 Academiestraat; its slender spire is considered by many to be the finest in the city. Built in the late Gothic style of the fifteenth century, local burghers and foreign traders met at this house. It was also the headquarters of the Society of the White Bear, which was responsible for arranging tournaments in the city. On the Academiestraat façade, to commemorate the society, a bear has been carved, one of the many figures decorating the niches. Brugeans are very fond of this bear, and he often wears a festive costume.

The Fine Arts Academy was founded at Poortersloge in 1739, and the street's name is a reference to it. In 1883, the Academy moved, and the building now accommodates state records.

Spanjaardstraat runs directly northward from the Academiestraat corner of the square. At **number 9**, Ignatius Loyola, founder of the Jesuit Order, stayed during the summers of 1528-30 on vacation from his studies in Paris.

Now a small hospital, **number 16** was built for a Spanish merchant in the sixteenth century. The Renaissance portal is a seventeenth-century addition.

Dated 1616, and also built for a Spanish merchant, Den Noodt Gods (Divine Providence) was the official name of **number 17**, but eventually it became better known as Het Spookhuis (The Haunted House), presumably because ghosts made appearances within; ironically, the Employment Office now occupies the building. It is an astonishingly late example of Gothic work, although the portal is Renaissance — giving the impression of an afterthought.

Return to Jan Van Eyckplein, from

Preceding page: A popular tourist destination even in winter, the streets of Bruges are brightly decorated for Christmas

the north-east corner of which runs Genthof. On the corner with the square, **number 1** is a castellated late-Gothic house. On the same side, at **number 7**, is a rare Bruges façade of timber (apart from its brick base).

Return to Jan Van Eyckplein and follow Spiegelrei, first left, which curves eastward following the canal. A vaguely Classical building at **number 13**, now a school, occupies the site of the former house of the English Trading Adventurers. In view of the importance of trade between Bruges and England it is a surprise to learn that the building only stood for 10 years. Ahead, cross **Koningbrug**, a hump-backed bridge of stone built in the fourteenth century, and from where are gained enchanting views of Poortersloge, the delicacy of which is enhanced by morning sunshine.

From the south side of the bridge, turn right and follow Spinola. Engelsestraat, first left, which runs southward (no need to enter it) was where the English Merchant Adventurers were permitted to build their own weigh-house, which stood here from the fourteenth to the sixteenth century.

Yet another return has been made to Jan Van Eyckplein, which is left this time from its south side, via Biskajersplein. This reference to Biscay indicates that we are back once more in the Spanish trading quarter, and at **number 6a** survives the former Den Struys, built in 1510 for Biscay merchants. Along its side appears a splendid Lombard frieze, a feature more usually associated with Romanesque architecture.

Wijnzakstraat runs southward from the square, and on the corner, at number 2, is **Huis de Croone**, a fifteenth-century mansion of four bays. Slender chimneys and brick ribs give an apparently greater height to what is already a tall building. Note the delicate trefoil Gothic tracery above the windows.

Wijnzakstraat runs into yet another small square, Sint Jansplein, where there is a four-sided lion's-head **water pump** of stone.

From Sint Jansplein follow Sint Jansstraat westward to Kraanplein, a square of no particular visual appeal but which was incorporated by Memling in his St John altarpiece, displayed in the Memling Museum. In the Middle Ages the municipal crane stood in this square, hence its name. Kraanplein leads to Vlamingstraat, left, and thence Markt.

South-West Brug

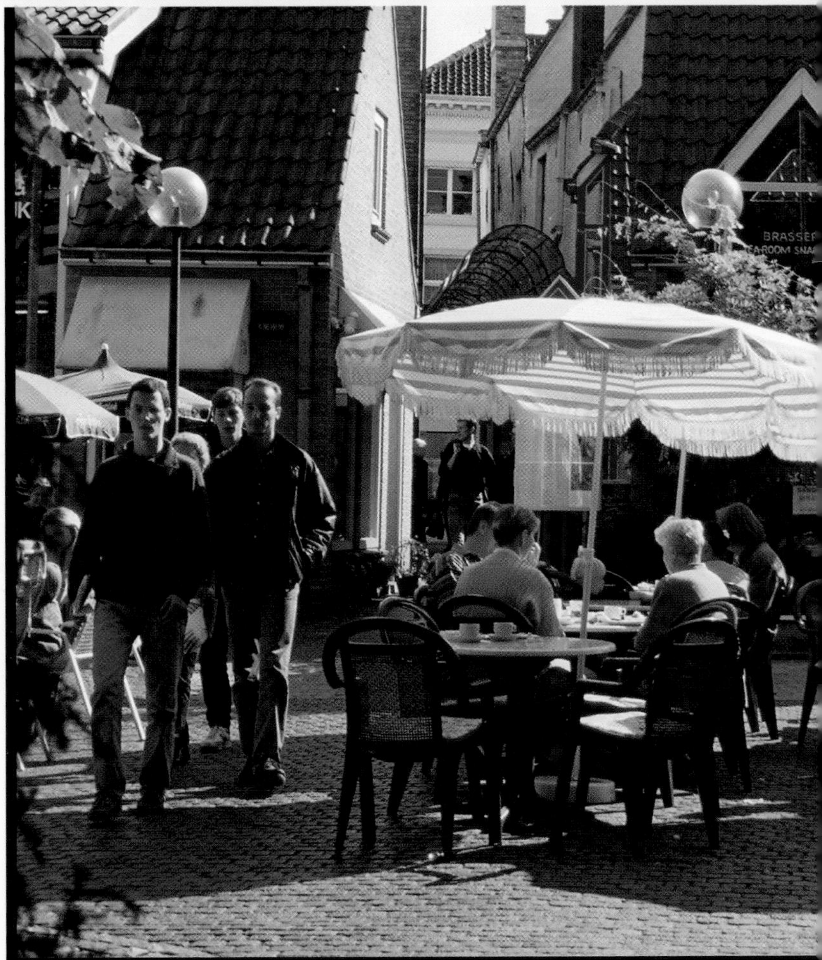

es

4

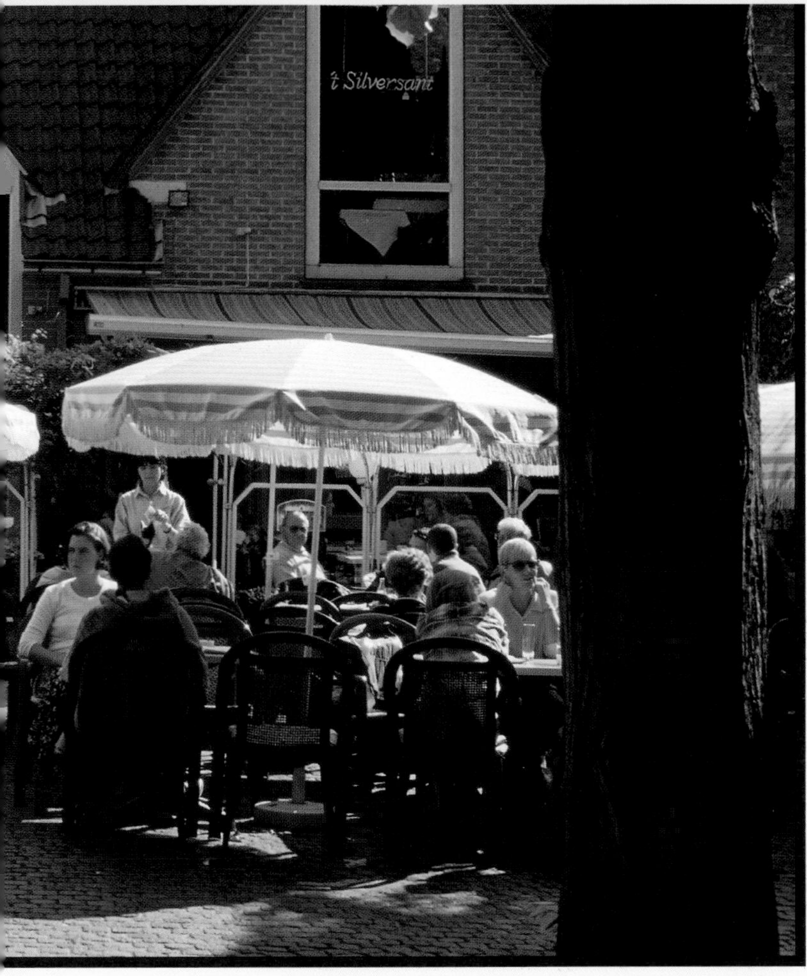

SHOPPING STREETS AND THE CATHEDRAL

Like the first itinerary, this one begins at **Markt** and ends at the station. It should not take long to complete, unless, of course, a great shopping expedition is planned. Apart from the shops, only the cathedral and two small chapels may be entered; fine weather is certainly an asset. Some may already have seen the cathedral, which is centrally located, but no detour is involved if it is included, as suggested, on this itinerary.

From Markt, follow Hallestraat, which runs south-eastward skirting the Gothic west range of **Halle**, built around 1365. Its arcade is basically Renaissance in concept, however, the windows above it remain Gothic. If wished access can be gained from the arcade to the central courtyard and Markt.

The name of Kartuizerinnenstraat, a continuation of Hallestraat, refers to the Carthusian monastery that formerly occupied much of it. A Baroque **archway** to the street serves as a memorial to Brugeans killed in both World Wars.

Continue ahead to the corner, where the church, built in 1612, is all that remains of the **Carthusian Convent**, founded in 1580. In the crypt are the ashes of Dachau concentration camp victims.

Return to Oude Burg, left, and proceed to **Hof van Watervliet**, at 27, where vestiges survive of the fifteenth-century mansion of Pieter Lanchals, executed by Brugeans in 1488 for supporting Archduke Maximilian's unpopular tax measures. The courtyard may be entered, but it will be seen that only the Gothic wings remain; the bulk of the mansion, to the south, has been completely rebuilt. It is known that Sir Thomas More and Erasmus visited the house in the sixteenth century, when it was the property of Marcus Laurinus, Dean of Sint Donaas Cathedral and an early humanist sympathiser.

Oude Burg terminates at **Simon Stevinplein**. Formerly a market square, the Westfleeshuis (West Meathouse) of the butchers stood here from the thirteenth century. Meat was sold from stalls set up outside the building. The bronze **Simon Stevin Monument**, erected in 1846, commemorates a man of many talents, who was born in Bruges in 1548. Primarily a mathematician, Stevin preceeded Galileo by 3 years in disproving Aristotle's theory that the speed of falling objects was determined by their weight. He also worked on applications of the decimal point, forecasting that all currenicies, weights and measurements would eventually be decimalised. Those British visitors who are still wedded to imperial measures are requested not to desecrate the monument! Equally important was Stevin's system of flooding by

Preceding pages: In spite of its northerly situation, Bruges has many al fresco cafés and restaurants sluices, which he devised as a defence measure for use in extreme circumstances: Stevin was also an engineer. This proved more applicable to Holland than Flanders, and Stevin emigrated to that country, serving as quartermaster in the army of Prince Maurits of Nassau. Stevin died in 1620.

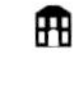

Steenstraat, the most fashionable shopping street in Bruges, runs parallel with Oude Burg, along the north side of Stevinplein. Many of its shops occupy ancient buildings, those of greatest architectural interest lying to the east of the square. On the north side, **number 40** was built in 1527 as the Shoemakers guildhouse. The guild's emblem, a high-heeled boot, is depicted on the gable. Strips of brickwork accentuate the vertical nature of the building, which stands on a low stone base. There are good examples of delicate Gothic tracery in brickwork above the windows.

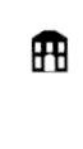

Adjoining, **number 38** is of much later construction, as is apparent from its Baroque appearance. Built in 1765 for the Carpenters Guild, the house would not seem out of place overlooking an Amsterdam canal.

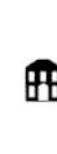

On the opposite side of Steenstraat, M&S has taken over **number 25**, a plaque on which is dated *Anno 1620*. This was originally built as the guildhouse of the Masons, and its present occupants must be congratulated on the immaculate appearance of the fresh-ly gilded and painted façade.

A short distance eastward, now part of Kreymborg, **number 19** was formerly the Bakers guildhouse. Its gable is dated 1650.

Return to Simon Stevinplein and turn, first right, into Kemelstraat. For most, the object of entering this short street now will be simply to establish the location of its famous tavern **'t Brugs Beertje**, at number 5. This is because it does not open until 4pm (not at all on Wednesdays) but the bar rarely closes before 1am.

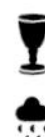

Mine host, Jan de Bruyne, is undoubtedly one of the country's greatest authorities on beer, stocking more than 300 Belgian varieties at all times. He and his expert staff seem to know exactly how each is brewed and from what raw materials. Customers will be informed immediately of the precise alcoholic rating of the ale selected, without a check being needed - apparently the barmen have memorised them all. At 't Brugs Beertje, beer is an extremely serious business, and the hushed tones normally adopted in a church seem to be appropriate. Here can be found the mysterious lambic beers, fermented with the natural yeast only found in 'the Brussels air'. These beers can be flavoured with raspberries or cherries, but they are also available unflavoured (white), when the taste is extremely sour. Lectures on beer take place from time to time in the venerable rear bar, usually on Wednesdays. Enthusiasts are welcome to attend and should check if there is an English language presentation during their stay.

From the 'cathedral of beer' to the cathedral of Bruges is only a few

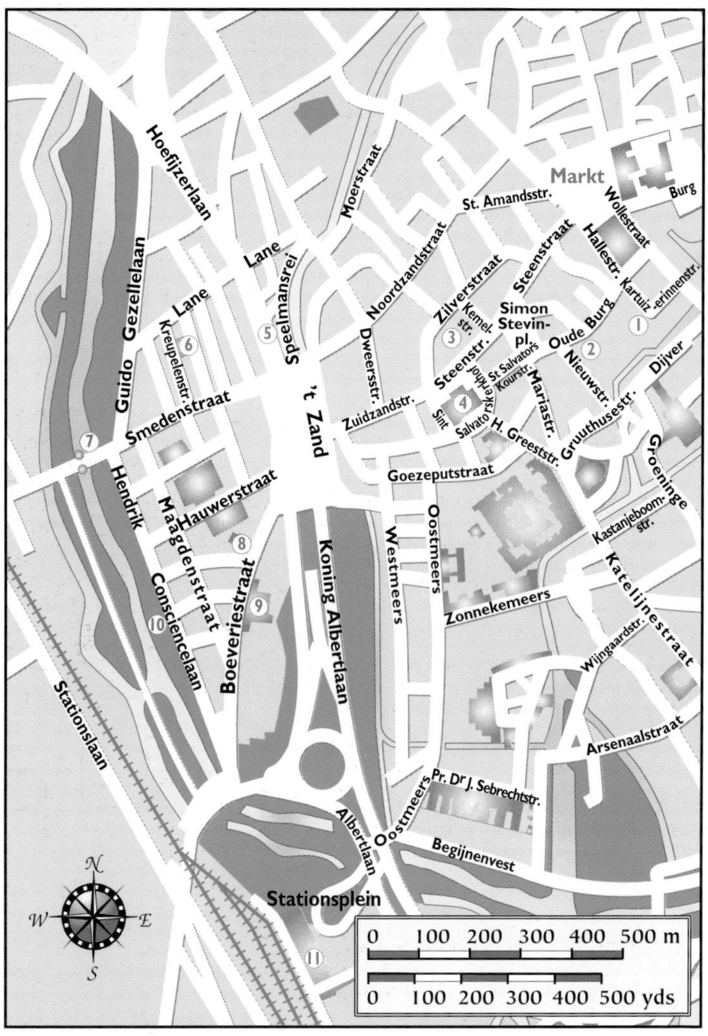

KEY

1. Former Carthusian Church
2. Hof van Watervliet (mansion)
3. 't Brugs Beertje (tavern)
4. Our Saviour's Cathedral (Sint Salvatorskathedraal)
5. Musicans Chapel (Speelmanskapel)
6. Our Lady's Chapel of the Blind (Blindekenskapel)
7. Smedenpoort (city gate)
8. Former Capucine Church
9. Abbey of St Godelieve
10. Waterhuis
11. Railway station and bus terminal

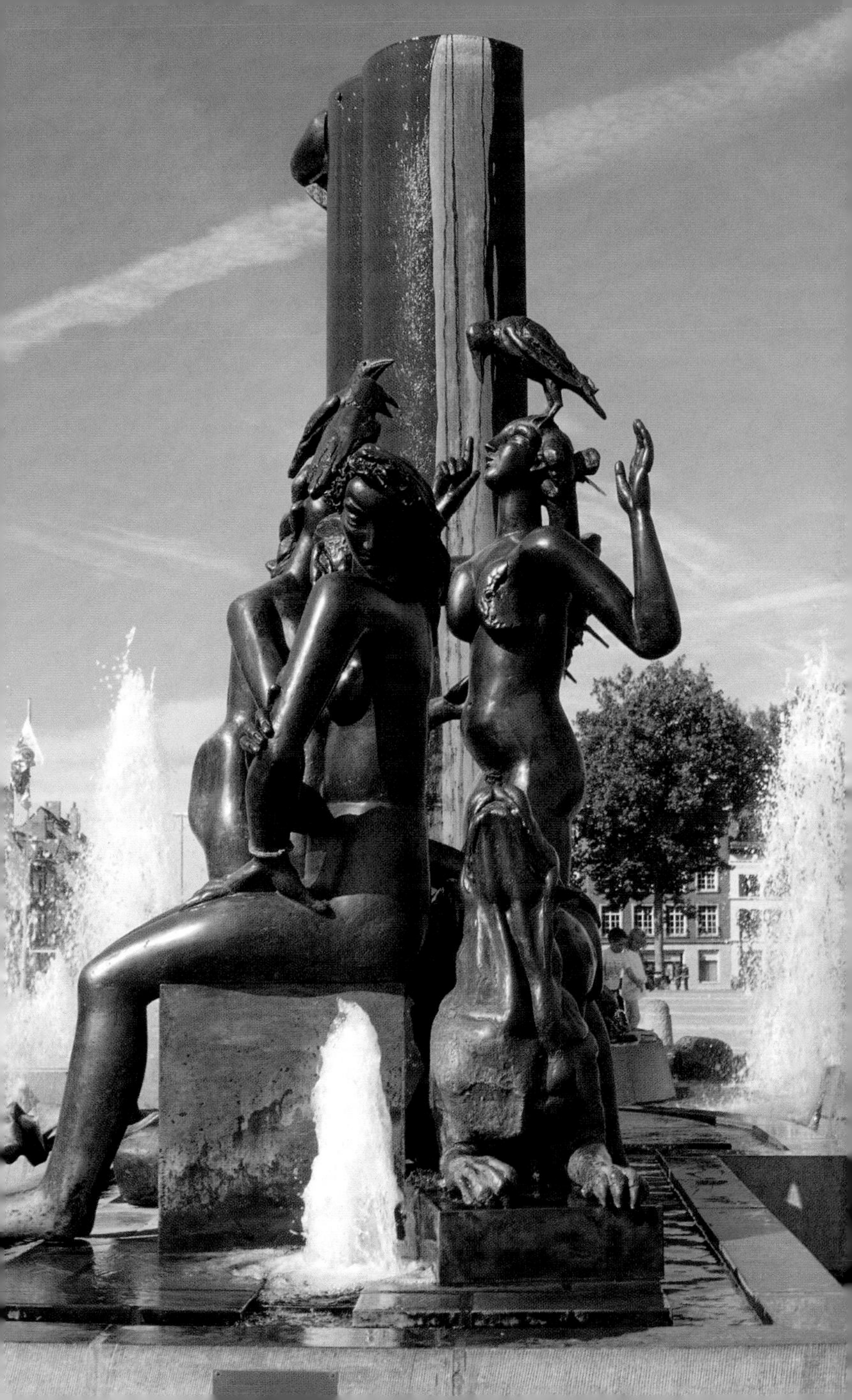

short steps away. Return to Steenstraat, right, and the great tower of **Sint Salvatorskathedraal** (Cathedral of Our Saviour) will be seen rising ahead from Sint Salvatorskerkhof, the square in which the cathedral stands.

Sint Salvatorskathedraal did not become the cathedral of Bruges until 1834, following Belgian independence. For more than 50 years, since the suppression of Sint Donaaskathedraal by the French iconoclasts, there had been no cathedral in the city. The church was probably founded in the ninth century, but its original building was completely destroyed by fire. All that survives of the church that replaced it in 1127 is the lower stone section of the tower. Its upper storey was lost in the fire of 1853, and rebuilt from funds donated by the English community in Bruges. Unfortunately, the British architect entrusted with the project, Robert Chantrell, decided to employ a neo-Romanesque style, the result being an unsatisfactory pastiche that had more in common with England's Norman churches than the Flemish tradition. It has been rebuilt more sympathetically in recent years.

The chancel and transepts were rebuilt in the mid-thirteenth century, and most of this work has survived; the present nave, however, was not completed until the early fifteenth century, and Jan van de Poele added chapels to the chancel's ambulatory in 1480.

Soaring brick vaults and an arcaded triforium at upper level, all with pointed arches, are unifying features of the entirely Flemish Gothic interior. In immediate contrast, on the west wall of the nave is the dynamic organ loft figure of the Almighty, a Baroque masterpiece by Artus Quellin, who carved it in 1682.

It may be recalled that the guildhouse of the Shoemakers has been seen in Steenstraat, identified by its high-heeled boot emblem. The same boot can be seen again in the east chapel of the cathedral's north transept, which was built for the Shoemakers Guild in 1372. Here, there are two boots (gilded and surmounted by a crown), one on either side of the Baroque altar of 1667.

Of greatest interest, however, is the chancel, where the Knights of the Order of the Golden Fleece attended a Chapter in 1478. Maximilian of Austria officiated, and Edward IV of England attended. The misericords of the stalls have been carved to commemorate the foundation of the Order. Above the stalls are the coats of arms of the knights who attended the Chapter. Edward IV's is the first from the left on the north side. The tapestries above the stalls were donated in the eighteenth century.

A series of late-Gothic fifteenth-century chapels punctuates the ambulatory around the chancel. Still a

Preceding page: Formerly the site of Bruges railway station, 't Zand now accommodates the Saturday market. This fountain, embellished with allegorical figures, is the most splendid in Bruges

mystery is the possessor of the monogram inscribed immediately right of the date, 1513, that appears on the screen to the first chapel on the north side.

Entered from the west wall of the south transept is the cathedral's **Museum**. Unfortunately, as in the Gruuthuse Museum, captions are in Dutch only. This is unfortunate, as there is much of interest to see, including treasures inherited from the old cathedral. To assist with dates, remember that *eeuw* is Dutch for century; *relikwieschrijn* means reliquary.

The museum is accommodated in a nineteenth-century cloister and the adjoining chapterhouse. Exceptional objects to look out for, and which should not drive foreign visitors mad trying to identify them, include: six huge medieval brasses from Sint Donaas; a Renaissance painting of the Virgin flanked by St Eloi and St Luke, by Lanceloot Blondeel, 1545; the silver reliquary of St Eloi, made by Jan Crabbe in 1612; the shrine of St Donaas; a copy of a lost portrait of Charles V (Keizer Karel), 1520, by Van Orley.

After leaving the cathedral proceed to the south side of its chancel and enter Heilige Geeststraat (Holy Ghost Street), which runs south-eastward from Sint Salvatorskerkhof. Immediately seen are two ancient buildings facing each other. **Hotel de Castillon**, right, at number 1, commemorates the fifteenth-bishop of Bruges, who lived here in 1743. At that time, the name of the house was Huyse 't Pauwkin (House of the Little Peacock), the peacock being a symbol of faith. Now a pension, **Geestelijk Hof**, opposite, at number 2, was formerly the residence of a regional representative, known as the Official of Tournai.

The **Bishop's Palace** has been located since 1834 at number 4 Heilige Geeststraat, the former Hof van Pittem. A monumental Baroque entrance leads to a large courtyard facing the Classical mansion, built in 1740. It is only open to those on official business.

Return to the cathedral's chancel and proceed anti-clockwise to Steenstraat, left. There are two buildings of particular interest in Zilverstraat, first right — for two different reasons. Until recently operating as the Vasquez restaurant, at **number 38**, the house behind its walled garden displays a gable of 1468. It was built for Jean Vasquez, who was the Spanish-born secretary to Isabella of Portugal, and accompanied her to Bruges when she married Philip the Good in 1430. Almost opposite, on the bend in the road, at 41, the **Zilveren Pauw** restaurant proclaimed on a plaque at the time of writing that its patron/chef, Patrick Devos, was 'Jeune Restaurateur d'Europe'.

Proceed through **Zilverpand**, the most ambitious covered shopping mall in Bruges, comprising fifty outlets grouped around a courtyard, and

Following page: Smedenpoort, a stone built gate in the south-west ramparts of the city

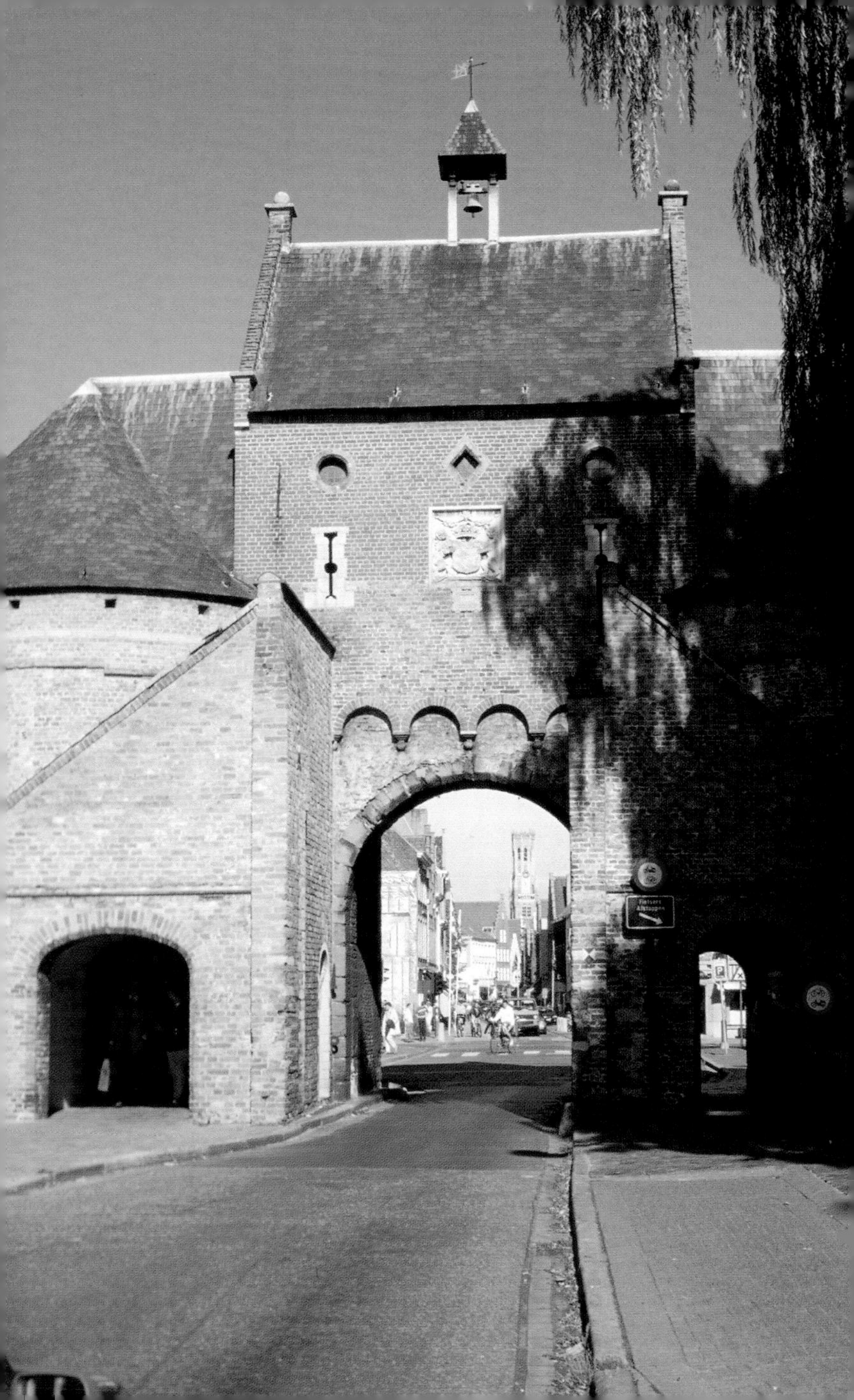

linking the north side of Zilverstraat with Noordzandstraat, left. Continue ahead to 't Zand, then turn immediately right along Speelmansrei, which follows the canal. This waterway is unusually narrow and leafy at this point, offering one of the most tranquil stretches in Bruges, which is surprising, considering its proximity to the busy 't Zand.

Overlooking the bridge, on the Beenhouwerstraat corner, is the tiny **Speelmanskapel** (Musicians Chapel), now an art gallery. The Guild of Musicians, which founded the chapel in 1421, acquired the exclusive right for its members to perform at official functions in the city — rather in the manner of a medieval 'Equity'. Large Gothic windows and a brass chandelier are the only features suggesting that the building was once a chapel.

Return to 't Zand via Speelmansrei once more (the parallel street is dreary).

In the thirteenth century, the horse and cattle market of Bruges was held in **'t Zand**; the square now accommodates the general Saturday market, which had been located in Markt until 1983, but a return to Markt is prophesied in the near future.

The first Bruges railway station opened at 't Zand in 1877, and trains continued to run through the square until after World War II, when the station was relocated to the south and the railway line diverted. It then became possible to extend 't Zand and lay out gardens on either side to the south; an underground car park (Centrum) for 1225 vehicles was excavated at the same time. Bars and restaurants with summer terraces line the east side of 't Zand, and are as popular with Brugeans as with tourists.

A splendid **fountain**, the finest in Bruges, was erected in 't Zand in 1986, the work of Stefaan Depuydt and Livia Canestraro. It is embellished by four sets of allegorical figures: bathing women represent the Flemish cities of Bruges, Antwerp, Ghent and Kortrijk; a horizontal, rather abstract form is meant to suggest the flat polders of the Flemish countryside (below this, on a plaque, are reproduced lines from Dante's Divine Comedy — a repetition of the Vlamingstraat quotation); fishermen are a reference to the industry of Belgium's North Sea, Zeebrugge in particular; finally, cyclists depict youth and hope for the future.

From the top of the fountain, peering in the direction of Damme, once the harbour of Bruges, is Tijl Uilenspiegel. He was a legendary figure, according to Belgians a Flemish hero who fought for independence.Under the name of Til Eulenspiegel, however, he is claimed by Germans to be no more than a fourteenth-century prankster, hailing from Schleswig Holstein. Internationally, Tijl Uilenspiegel is better known under his German name due to Richard Strauss's composition of 1894 dedicated to him.

Smedenstraat runs westward from the north-west corner of 't Zand. It is a continuation of Noordzandstraat, and, like that street, a popular shopping thoroughfare - particularly good for food. Follow Kreupelenstraat, fourth right, to the small chapel, at number 8. Approached from the alleyway beside the chapel, the **Blindekenskapel** (Our Lady's Chapel of the Blind) is entered from its side door. Happily, the building always seems to be open during the day.

Following the Battle of the Pevelenberg, in 1304, the Flemish gave thanks to the Virgin Mary for their victory over the French, by promising to build an almshouse for blind, destitute citizens of Bruges. This is commemorated every year on the morning of 15 August by the Procession of the Promise, in which a votive candle, weighing 30lbs, is paraded through the streets from the Blindekens chapel to Onze-Lieve-Vrouw ter Potterie in north-east Bruges — quite a weight for such a distance. The chapel, probably founded in the fifteenth century, was rebuilt in 1652 and a new canopied pulpit made for it. Opposite this pulpit, in a silver niche, stands a wooden, part-gilded *Virgin and Child* statue. Below this, the sixteenth-century *Calvary relief* was presented by Francis van Busleiden, Dean of St Donaas.

Suspended from a beam is a model of the three-master merchant ship, *St Michael*, which miraculously docked at Bruges loaded with grain during the famine of 1588 — immediately after prayers to end the famine had been said in this chapel, so it is claimed.

Return to Smedenstraat, right, and continue ahead to **Smedenpoort**, the gateway spanning the road. Built of stone in 1368, but remodelled in 1615, Smedenpoort is contemporary with Ezelpoort, the next gate in the ramparts to the north. The bell was rung as a warning whenever the gate was about to be opened or closed. A small bronze skull, set in the gate on the Smedenstraat side, is a reminder of the Brugean traitor who was executed in 1688 for attempting to open the gate for the besieging army of Louis XIV.

Return to the west side of 't Zand, which is still known as Vrijdagmarkt (the Friday Market, which was closed in 1939), and proceed southward to Boeveriestraat, second right. Due to its peripheral situation, **Boeveriestraat**, one of the most historic of all Bruges thoroughfares, is neglected by the majority of visitors. Many of its buildings are almshouses, identified by their date and owner's name. Even numbers are on the west side.

The **Hotel Sofitel**, at number 4, incorporates the façade of the former Capucine Convent, including its chapel.

Opposite, at number 5, the **Van Campen almshouse** of 1436 is linked by a similar building to another important range, the **Van Peenen almshouse** of 1629, which occupies 9-19.

Entered through a brick archway to its forecourt, **number 18**, on the opposite side of the road, is the former monastery of the Capucine friars.

Facing Fonteinstraat, at 45, the **Abbey of St Godelieve** was built in 1623. Above the entrance, in a niche, is a bust of St Godelieve. Strangled and then, just to make sure, thrown into a well by her husband Bertholf van Gistel, Godelieve was canonized in 1084. The original abbey dedicated to her and constructed in the town of Gistel, came under threat from Protestants in 1578 and was abandoned by the nuns, who walked the 21km (13 miles) to Bruges, where they settled the following year. The abbey was sold at the French Revolution, in 1796, but regained by the nuns 4 years later.

From the entrance it is usually possible to view the interior of the church. At its consecration, in 1623, *The Coronation of the Virgin* painting was donated by Monseigneur Dionysius Christophon. His patron saint, St Dyonysius more usually referred to as St Denis, is depicted on the right.

Maagdenstraat joins Boeveriestraat on its west side, where a small square, Joris Dumeryplein, is formed. Here, protected by great planks of oak, is the **Dumery Bell**, named to commemorate the Dumery family, which cast it in their foundry nearby. The bell was brought here from Markt, where it had been rung in the Belfry to warn citizens whenever a major fire broke out in the city.

Van Voldenstraat, a short street, leads westward from Joris Dumeryplein to Hendrik Consciencelaan, which borders part of the open green belt that surrounds most of the city. A footpath leads to the **Waterhuis**, built in the fifteenth century as Boeverievest, a pumping station for the city's water supply; horses operated a chain pump to draw water from the canal. In 1760, that Waterhuis was superseded by a new one, located between the inner and outer canals. Adapted to steam in 1893, the station was closed and demolished in 1925.

Return to Boeveriestraat and continue southward.

The west side of Boeveriestraat ends with its longest almshouse, **Godshuis de Moor**, which stretches from numbers 52 to 76. Donaas de Moor and his wife Ariana de Vos founded the thirteen-dwelling almshouse in 1480. The Carpenters, Coopers and Masons guilds were each allocated three units, the other four being given to the Sint Juliaanshospitaal, opposite, for the use of their staff. Coats of arms of the three guilds and the hospital identify each house.

De Moor was accused of supporting Maximilian of Austria, at the time imprisoned in Craenenburg, and had to flee Bruges in 1488. He died in exile at Middlelburg.

The **Sint Juliaanshospitaal** formerly occupied number 73. It was founded in 1290 to provide accommodation for travellers and the destitute by the Filles Dieu, nuns from Arras in France. They were later assisted by the Sint Juliaan brotherhood. Later, the establishment became a mental home, and cared for patients until 1900. Two paintings by Memling, presented to the hospital, are exhibited in the Memling Museum.

From around 1300 to 1883, Boeveriepoort, a gateway in the ramparts, ended Boeveriestraat. It was rebuilt in 1367 but, following the battle between Brugeans and Philip the Good, the Duke of Burgundy closed it to traffic between 1438 and 1452, during which period the gate served as a chapel. Reopened once more, the now dilapidated structure was rebuilt in 1807, but it was demolished in 1863 and no trace remains.

A left turn at the approach to Boeveriebrug leads to Albertlaan and Stationsplein, right, for the railway and bus stations.

Additional Information

Place to Visit

Cathedral of Our Saviour Museum
St Salvatorskerkhof
Open: 1 April-30 September 10-11.30am, 2-5pm. Sunday 3-5pm. Closed Wednesday.
1 October-31 March 2-5pm. Closed on Wednesday, Sunday and holidays.

Damme

Lying just 7km (4 miles) to the north of Bruges, Damme can be reached from the city by bus or boat (see page 139-140 Facts for Visitors). It is a delightful, unspoilt Flemish village, found-ed in the twelfth century to provide the outer harbour of Bruges. By tradition, a breach in the dam at this point was repaired by filling it with the corpse of a black dog, killed for the purpose. The dam workers then settled nearby, calling their new village Dam of the Dog.

Although classed as a village, Damme has its own Gothic church and town hall, a market square and a medieval hospital. As Damme is approached, either by road or canal, the high tower of Onze-Lieve-Vrouwekerk is the first building seen. Beneath the porch of its tower is buried Jacob van Maerlant, regarded as the father of Flemish poetry, and a Damme resident during the second half of the thirteenth century. Overlooking Marktplein is the Town Hall (Stadhuis), a fifteenth century, late-Gothic building, decorated at upper level with carvings representing the counts of Flanders. Standing in the square is a statue of Jacob van Maerlant, the poet.

The Tourist Office is located in the Town Hall. By tradition, Tijl Uilenspiegel, the legendary hero, was born in Damme (see page 127).

Charles the Bold married for the third time in 1468, his bride being Margaret of York, sister of England's King Edward IV. The civil wedding took place in the manor house of Damme magistrate Eustaas Wyte, and the building has survived. Also of interest in Damme is the ancient St John's hospital and the old windmill.

Facts for Visitors

Accommodation

A map showing the location of all recommended accommodation can be found on page 14. Accommodation of all kinds can be difficult to obtain in Bruges outside the winter months, particularly in August, when important festivals are held. The Belgian Tourist Board will provide an illustrated list of hotels, bed and breakfast establishments and camping sites on request, and advance booking is advisable. Hotels are categorized from one to four stars, but all rooms, whatever their grade, will have private toilet and shower facilities. Bruges is a compact city, and the advantage of a reasonably central location is obvious. Room tariffs are not dissimilar from equivalent British accommodation. Many will be attracted by the hotels that have been adapted from century-old houses, some of which retain period features and are furnished with antiques.

For those arriving at Bruges without pre booking, a free hotel reservation service is provided at the railway station and the central tourist office in Burg.

Recommended Hotels

The following hotels and guest-houses are all centrally located.

Four Star

Brughe (ter)
2, Oost Gistelhof
☎ 34 03 24 Fax: 33 88 73

Bryghia
4, Oosterlingenplein
☎ 33 80 59 Fax: 34 14 30
This is a small, exquisitely furnished period building, which was originally connected with the Hanseatic League's Bruges headquarters.

Holiday Inn Crowne Plaza
10, Burg
☎ 34 58 34 Fax: 34 56 15
An ultra modern hotel overlooking the Town Hall. Its basement incorporates fragments of the old cathedral. Facilities include a swimming pool and a sauna.

Navarra
41, St Jakobsstraat
☎ 34 05 61 Fax: 33 67 90
As its name suggests, the building was formerly the Trading House of the Navarre merchants.

Orangerie (De)
10, Kartuizerinnenstraat
☎ 34 16 49 Fax: 33 30 16
The Orangerie is one of the most centrally located hotels in the city and, although small, very highly regarded for its standard of service and beautifully proportioned rooms.

Relais Oud Huis Amsterdam
3, Spiegelrei
☎ 34 26 90 Fax: 33 88 91
Overlooks the tranquil Spiegelrei canal and the medieval Poortersloge.

Three Star

Adornes
26, Sint Annarei
☎ 34 13 36 Fax: 34 20 85
Occupying a step-gabled sixteenth-century building, the Adornes has rooms with views over the adjacent inner canal.

Duc de Bourgogne
12, Huidenvettersplein
☎ 33 20 38 Fax: 34 40 47
Another centrally located canal side hotel.

Grand Hotel Oude Burg
5, Oude Burg
☎ 44 51 11 Fax: 44 51 00
A large, modern hotel, the Grand is located immediately behind the Belfry.

Two Star

Cordoeanier
18, Cordoeanierstraat
☎ 33 90 51 Fax: 34 61 11
This is the most conveniently located of all the two-star hotels in Bruges.

Europ
18, Augustijnenrei
☎ 33 79 75 Fax: 34 52 66
Augustijnenrei is generally regarded as the prettiest of all Bruges canals.

Imperial
24, Dweersstraat
☎ 33 90 14
Although a small hotel, the Imperial's rooms are well-equipped. Its building is step-gabled.

Lucca
30, Naaldenstraat
☎ 34 20 67 Fax: 33 34 64
Fourteenth-century rooms survive in this friendly, family-run hotel, once the trading house of the Italian merchants from Lucca.

Salvators
7, Sint Salvatorskerkhof
☎ 33 19 21 Fax: 33 94 64
Accommodated in another period building, Hotel Salvators lies directly behind the cathedral.

Voermanshuys ('t)
14, Oude Burg
☎ 34 13 96 Fax: 34 23 90
Within a short walk of all the major sights of Bruges.

One Star

Ibis Brugge Centrum
65a, Katelijnestraat
☎ 33 75 75 Fax: 33 64 19
All 128 rooms have private WC, bath and shower. The Ibis is located in one of the city's major shopping streets - a little to the south of centre.

Koffieboontje ('t)
4, Hallestraat
☎ 33 80 27 Fax: 34 39 04
The hotel is small but its outstandingly central position, rare in this hotel grade, and well-fitted rooms will suit many.

Putje ('t)
31, 't Zand
☎ 33 28 47 Fax: 34 14 23
Also a small hotel, the rooms of 't Putje are most comfortable. Slightly to the west of the city centre.

'H' Grade

Central
30, Markt
☎ 33 18 05 Fax: 34 68 78
Reasonably priced, no hotel in Bruges could be more central than the Central, facing south over the city's main square.

Patritius
11, Riddersstraat
☎ 33 84 54 Fax: 33 96 34
Very centrally located, rooms are fresh and well appointed.

Guest Houses

Mrs Deloof
14, Gheerwijnstraat
☎ 34 05 44

Mr and Mrs Gheeraert
9, Riddersstraat
☎ 33 56 27

Mrs Nyssen
50, Moerstraat
☎ 34 31 71

Mrs de Vriese
40, Predikherenstraat
☎ 33 42 24

Youth Accommodation

International Youth Hostel Europa
Baron Ruzettelaan 143
8310 Assebroek
☎ 050 35 26 79
42 rooms

Bauhaus International Youth Hostel
135-137 Langestraat
8-8000 Brugge
☎ (050) 34 10 93
19 rooms

Credit Cards

Virtually all establishments accept leading credit cards.

Customs Regulations

Belgium is, of course, a member of the European Union, and the usual EU duty free allowances apply. At the time of writing, these allowances are scheduled to remain in operation until 1999. One litre of duty free spirits may be purchased on route to Belgium, and a similar quantity on the return journey; it is not permitted to purchase both bottles on the same occasion. Only marginal savings are made on duty free tobacco products, as they are extremely cheap in Belgium itself, as local taxes on them are low.

There is no limit to what may be brought back from Belgium, and tobacco products are the best buy for smokers, particularly loose tobacco, which is sold in 50 gramme packets as in the United Kingdom (in France the packs are 40 grammes).

There is little point in buying wine or spirits in Belgium as little saving will be made. Beer, however, is another matter. Prices are very much lower than in the United Kingdom, but cans or bottles of beer are bulky and, unless travelling with a vehicle, this will be a limiting factor on how much is purchased. As with tobacco, only sufficient for personal consumption will be permitted.

A leaflet explaining the situation is obtainable at all embarkation ports.

Electricity

Voltage in Belgium is 220 AC. Twin-point sockets are universal, but as these do not quite accept British twin-point plugs a continental adaptor is necessary. A single adaptor that converts British three-point and two-point plugs to continental two-point sockets is recommended.

Festivals and Events

Exit, published monthly, lists each month's attractions in the city; it can be obtained free in advance from Belgian Tourist Offices or on arrival in Bruges.

Major Events

Ascension Day (mid May) Procession of the Holy Blood. An ancient Bruges tradition, the procession through the streets of Bruges to the Holy Blood Basilica in Burg celebrates the arrival of the relic in the city.

July/August: Flanders Festival of Early Music

15 August: Blindekens Procession. Established 700 years, the procession leads from the Blindekens Chapel to Our Lady of the Potterie.

August (second half): Festival of the Canals. Held every 3 years, performances at various canal-side locations take place over six evenings. Tableaux are illuminated, and performances begin at 9pm, each being repeated at 15 minute intervals. It takes 3 hours to reach all of them on foot.

August: Pageant of the Golden Tree. Held every 5 years since 1958, this pageant takes place on two consecutive evenings. Around 100 groups take part in both 2-hour long performances. Primarily, the pageant commemorates the marriage of Charles the Bold and Margaret of York in 1468. High spots are the arrival of the groom in Bruges and a 'medieval' tournament held in Markt.

Getting to Bruges

Visitors from the United Kingdom are able to reach Bruges via ferry, air or train. Although Bruges is a short distance from the North Sea coast, passenger services to Belgium are now very restricted, Zeebrugge only being served from Hull and Ostend from Ramsgate (ferry or jetfoil). Alternatively, those who are on a tight budget or enjoy a sea trip may travel from Dover to Calais and proceed from there to Bruges by train, changing at Lille. Motorists can take advantage of the Channel Tunnel via 'Le Shuttle' trains. From 1996, buses direct to Bruges will connect with Eurostar services at Lille International Station.

Direct flights operate from several UK airports to Brussels and Antwerp, a 30 minute journey; trains from either city take approximately an hour to Bruges.

Eurostar trains, via the Channel Tunnel, make the uninterupted 3¼ hour journey between London Waterloo International Station and either Lille Europe Station, for direct buses to Bruges, or Brussels Midi Station, from where there are fast train services to Bruges. From January 1996, some trains could be joined at Ashford International Station, thus reducing the journey by almost one hour. Apart from its speed and convenience, the great advantage of the Channel Tunnel to most is the guarantee that neither their equanimity nor their schedule will be disturbed by inclement weather. In 1995, bargain fares for two holidaymakers travelling together were introduced, which included the onward journey from Brussels to Bruges (or anywhere else in Belgium).

HEALTH

Most travel insurance policies provide adequate health cover. All EU countries have reciprocal health service arrangements, but visitors must bring with them an EIII certificate to obtain treatment under the scheme; it is available from all post offices. For emergency medical service in Bruges at weekends ☎ 81 38 99; during weekday nights ☎ 51 63 76.

MEASUREMENTS

Metric measurements operate in Belgium. Whilst most UK visitors will be familiar with them, it may help some to remember that 1 kilometre equals approximately ⅔ of a mile, 1 kilogram weighs just over 2lb, 100 grammes is approximately ¼lb and 1 litre is slightly less than two pints.

MONEY

One Belgian franc is divided into 100 *centimes*, but only 50 *centime* coins are current. As a member of the European Monetary Union, Belgian currency is, in effect, linked to the *Deutschmark*, and in consequence the Belgian *franc* has remained stable for some years.

There are many exchange points in the city, and most hotels will change money and travellers cheques, although usually at an unfavourable rate. An exchange desk, which operates in the same office as the Tourist Office, is open daily in the season, and at weekends only in winter. Banks give the best rates and are open Monday to Friday 9am-12noon and 2-4pm; some larger branches may also open Saturday mornings. Although convenient, Eurocheques are not accepted by all, and the rate given by the issuing bank is rarely advantageous. Bank notes are issued in the following denominations of Belgian *francs*: 100, 500, 1,000, 2,000, 10,000. Coins are minted in 1, 5, 20 and 50 Belgian *franc* denominations.

Opening Times of Museums and Churches

Specific opening times are given for locations throughout the book. Museums in Bruges formerly closed for 2 hours at lunch but no longer do so. Every church in Bruges is closed from 12noon-2pm. The most important church in Bruges, Onze-Lieve-Vrouwekerk, is shut from 11.30am-2pm. Some churches, such as Sint Annakerk, open only for half an hour before services during the winter. In the summer they also open in the late afternoon or evening eg Sint Gilleskerk and Sint Walburgakerk. Visitors should show great discretion during services, preferably returning later unless taking part.

A combined entry ticket for the Brangwyn, Groeninge, Gruuthuse and Memling museums is available, at a reduced rate, from the Tourist Office or any of the four museums in question.

Passports

A current full passport is required from all those entering Belgium, whether or not they are from an EU member country.

Postage

Postage stamps may be purchased from many small shops, including book shops and tobacconists, in addition to Post Offices. Post Offices are open Monday to Friday 9am-12noon and 2-5pm. Pillar boxes are red, as in the United Kingdom.

Public Convenience

Virtually all public toilets in Bruges are manned by women; they will insist on a fixed payment of 10 BF being made in advance by both sexes.

Public Holidays

On public holidays, virtually all shops and banks are closed. These are: New Year's Day, Easter Monday, 1 May, Ascension Day (mid May), All Saints Day (1 November) Armistice Day (11 November), Christmas Day. Flemish National Holiday, 11 July, and Independence Day, 21 July, are also holidays for banks and public offices, but shops remain open.

Restaurants

A map showing the location of recommended restaurants can be found on page 14.

The following restaurants are recommended, but should not be regarded as an exclusive selection. Price categories must be regarded as very approximate.

Over 2,000 BF

Duc de Bourgogne
12, Huidenvettersplein
☎ 33 20 38
This top class hotel serves high quality French cuisine in its canalside restaurant.

Kapittel ('t)
10, Burg
☎ 34 58 34
The restaurant specializes in gastronomic weekends.

Karmeliet (De)
19, Langestraat
☎ 33 82 59
Classical French cuisine, fish dishes in particular.

Snippe (De)
53, Nieuwe Gentweg
☎ 33 70 70
Definitely the tops in quality and price. French dishes are served in a most delightful dining room. Fish specialities.

Swaene (Die)
1, Steenhouwersdijk
☎ 34 27 98
Gourmets should not miss this classic French restaurant.

Zilveren Pauw (Patrick Devos)
41, Zilverstraat
☎ 33 55 66
Patrick Devos, voted young restauranteur of the year, prepares innovative dishes, with many fish specialities.

1,200 - 2,000 BF

Bhavani
5, Simon Stevinplein
☎ 33 90 25
At the time of writing, this is the only Indian restaurant in Bruges. Quality is good but the prices are high, due, presumably, to lack of competition.

Braamberg (Den)
11, Pandreitje
☎ 33 73 70
Delicious lamb and fish specialities are the highlights of Braamberg's classic cuisine.

Kasteel Minnewater
4, Minnewaterpark
☎ 34 42 54
Set in a nineteenth-century Gothic fantasy castle, this restaurant overlooks the romantic lake. A vast summer terrace.

Lotteburg
43, Goezeputstraat
☎ 33 75 35
Another top class restaurant specialising in fish.

Paspartout (De)
1, Jeruzalemstraat 1
☎ 34 66 13
Also good for large parties, game is served in season.

Spinola
1, Spinolarei
☎ 45 17 85
Set in a pretty period house, there are several lamb specialities — and a renowned apple tart.

Tanuki
3, Noordstraat
☎ 34 75 12
A Japanese restaurant with the usual Japanese dishes — *sushi* and *sashimi* are first rate.

Visscherie (De)
8, Vismarkt
☎ 33 02 12
As may be expected, fish is the speciality here. A definitive *waterzooi* is served.

700 - 1,200 BF

Begijntje ('t)
11, Walstraat
☎ 33 00 89
This tiny restaurant, with only 20 covers, serves regional dishes and reliably tender steaks.

Belle Epoque
43, Zuidzandstraat
☎ 33 18 72
Regional dishes concentrate on fish dishes.

Central
30, Markt
☎ 33 18 05
Definitely not a tourist trap in spite of its Markt location, Central offers a varied menu at reasonable prices.

Keteltje ('t)
20, Oude Burg
☎ 34 86 20
An old-established Bruges restaurant, 't Keteltje offers regional specialties.

Maximilian van Oostenrijk
17, Wijngaardplein
☎ 33 47 23
Charcoal grills.

Oud Brugge
33, Kuipersstraat
☎ 33 54 02
Particularly good for large parties (karaoke facilities). Meals are served in a vaulted thirteenth-century cellar.

Sint-Joris
29, Markt
☎ 33 30 62
This is another Markt restaurant that can be recommended. Excellent fish *waterzooi* and eels are the specialities.

Below 700 BF

China
45, Zuidzandstraat
☎ 33 21 54
This basically Chinese restaurant also serves an acceptable Indonesian *rijsttafel* — primarily, one supposes, to please visitors from Holland, where this dish is popular, even though it is rarely prepared with sufficient chillies.

Due Venezie (Le)
2, Kleine Sint-Amandsstraat
☎ 33 23 26
Probably the best Italian restaurant in Bruges.

Michelangelo
16, O.L.V.Kerkhof Zuid
☎ 33 38 93
Seasonal and fish dishes.

Pallieterke ('t)
28, 't Zand
☎ 34 01 77
Eel, steaks and regional dishes are popular.

Raadskelder
21, Eiermarkt
☎ 34 31 32
Mussels are rated among the best in Bruges.

Voske Malpertuus ('t)
9, Eiermarkt
☎ 33 30 38
Superb *waterzooi* is served in two helpings. One room is a medieval cellar.

Telephones

Virtually all telephone booths in Bruges only accept cards, but one coin box survives in the hallway of the Tourist Office. Phone cards can be purchased at similar outlets to postage stamps. From Belgium, the dialling code for the United Kingdom is 00441, then dial the number omitting the initial 0 of the local code. For USA and Canada 001, and Eire 00353. To telephone Bruges from abroad dial 003250, followed by the number.

Time

In the winter, Belgium is one hour ahead of Greenwich Meantime, but two hours ahead from March to October. It is expected that the time change will shortly coincide with British Summertime.

Tipping

The service charge is always included in hotel and restaurant bills, and additional gratuities are not expected. However, for very exceptional service, a small additional amount is welcomed. No tips to taxi drivers, boat excursion commentators nor horse-drawn cab drivers are necessary.

Transport

Taxis

On arrival, many will take a taxi from the station to their hotel — and be astonished by the enormous fare demanded; this is partly because the driver's return to base must be paid for. Belgian tariffs are among the highest in the world — it is most unlikely that the visitor is being cheated. For those to whom the cost of fares is unimportant, there is another rank in Markt, and hotels, of course, will book cabs for their clients when the charge will be even more horrendous. No taxis are permitted to ply for hire.

Buses

Staff at the local bus information kiosk outside the station will advise on which bus route passes a required address in Bruges. If several bus journeys are anticipated, a ten-journey pass (Stadskaart) should be purchased from the kiosk, which reduces the total cost by almost 50 per cent. As Bruges is so compact, and its narrow streets can only be viewed sensibly on foot, few bus journeys will be needed within the city, apart from returning from the station at the end of the two southbound itineraries suggested in this book. However, it should be borne in mind that most will have to make a trip to the station for their homeward journey via Brussels, and some, in addition, will wish to make several train journeys from Bruges to other parts of Belgium, which will necesitate more bus journeys to the station.

In the summer, those who plan to visit Damme, Ostend or Zeebrugge by regional buses, can board them either at Stationplein or 't Zand. In winter, there is no public transport to Damme, but Zeebrugge can always be reached by train.

Boats

Popular boat trips to Damme from April to September run from Noorweegse Kaai in north Bruges. To reach the boarding point take bus 4 from Markt.

Trips along the Bruges canals run daily 1 March to 30 November from 10am-6pm. In December and February they operate only at weekends; there are several boarding points, beginning south of Burg, and each trip lasts 30 minutes. The tariff from 1996 is 170 BF.

Horse-Drawn Cabs

These depart from Burg and proceed to the Begijnhof, where a short pause is made before returning. Up to 4 passengers can be accommodated, and in 1996 the 30 minute tour cost 800 BF for the cab, irrespective of the number of occupants.

Taxis

From the only railway station in Bruges, situated at Stationsplein, trains depart for all major destinations in Belgium. There are frequent services to Ostend, Zeebrugge and Ghent, and the journey time to each should not exceed 20 minutes.

It must be said that due to its extreme westerly location, Bruges is not the most convenient base from which to make nationwide tours. Belgium, however, is a small country, and as long as an early start is made, day trips from Bruges are possible to Antwerp, Brussels, the Ardennes — and even Luxembourg at a push.

Many visitors will have journeyed to Bruges via Brussels (approximately 50 minutes by inter city trains), and some may find it more convenient to coincide a Brussels trip with the first or last day of their holiday — thus saving time and money. Left luggage facilities are provided at both Brussels Midi Station (for the Channel Tunnel) and Brussels Central Station, which is more convenient for visiting the city - the stations are close to each other and on the same route from Bruges.

It is imperative that intercity (ic) trains are taken whenever possible, otherwise journeys can become very tedious. Stopping trains are indicated by L. If a great deal of rail travel is envisaged, some may find it convenient to purchase a B-Tourrail ticket, which offers unlimited travel throughout the Belgian rail network for varying numbers of days as required during a one month period. A second class 5 day ticket cost 995 BF in 1996. However, if day trips to just one destination per day, eg Antwerp or Brussels, are made, the cost saving will not be great.

Bicycle Hire

The flatness of most of Belgium has resulted in the country becoming popular with cyclists. Bruges encourages cycling by permitting bicycles to be ridden in each direction along streets that are one-way only to motor vehicles. Some hotels loan tricycles to their clients. Hiring points are as follows: Luggage Department, Railway Station, Stationsplein; 't Koffieboontje, Hallestraat 4; Eric Popelier, Hallestraat 14 (also scooters); De Ketting, Gentpoortsraat 23.

Motoring

Those with large families — or a large car boot in which to pack crates of beer — may wish to drive to Bruges. Few UK visitors will not appreciate that everywhere on the continent vehicles drive on the right side of the road, give priority to vehicles approaching from the right, and proceed anti-clockwise at roundabouts. UK motorists in Belgium must, by law, display a GB sticker and keep with them in their car a red triangle, for use as a breakdown warning if needed, and a basic first-aid kit. Whilst not a legal requirement, a green card for third party insurance is recommended.

Once having arrived in Bruges, the car should be parked as soon as possible. There are underground car parks at 't Zand, Zilverpand and Biekorf, all of which charge. However, the largest car park, which is entered beside the station, makes no charge.

Strangers will find driving within the ancient city of Bruges to be a nightmare, with around 50 ever-changing one-way streets to be negotiated. For the brave, remember that free parking is permitted in a blue zone, but only for the time indicated, and a parking disc, obtainable from any service station, must always be displayed showing the arrival time. Spaces in blue zones are extremely hard to obtain. Parking metres are expensive and can never be used for more than 3 hours.

Between 7pm and 9am, and throughout Sundays and bank holidays, unlimited parking is free in blue zones and at metres.

Useful Addresses and Telephone Numbers

Belgian Tourist Offices

England
29 Princes Street
London W1R 7RG
☎ 0171 629 3977

USA
Suite 1501
780 Third Avenue
New York
NY 10017
☎ (212) 7588130

City Tourist Office
Burg 11, B-8000
Bruges
☎ 44 86 86
Open: 1 October to 31 March, Monday to Friday 9.30am-5pm, Saturday 9.30am-1pm and 2-5.30pm.
1 April to 30 September, Monday to Friday 9.30am-6.30pm, Saturday, Sunday and Public Holidays 10am-12noon and 2-6.30pm.

Railway Station
1 October to 31 March, Monday to Friday 10am-5.30pm, Saturday 9.30am-5.30pm.
1 April to 30 September, Monday to Saturday 10.30am-6.30pm.

Police Station
Hauwerstraat 7
☎ 44 88 44

Railway Station
Stationsplein
☎ 38 24 06 or 38 23 82

Bus Information
☎ 0800 13663

Index